EDITED BY

RONALD J. SIDER

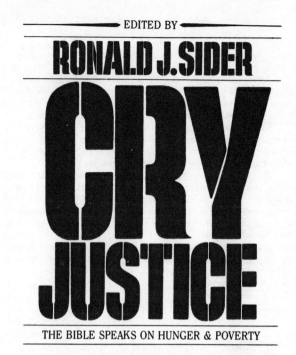

CRY JUSTICE

THE BIBLE SPEAKS ON HUNGER & POVERTY

A BREAD FOR THE WORLD READER

D0838397

InterVarsity Press
Downers Grove
Illinois 60515

Acknowledgements

A wide variety of Protestant and Catholic biblical scholars and theologians read the manuscript and offered their critical evaluation. They cannot be blamed for the remaining deficiencies, but there are fewer because of their wise advice.

Three friends who gave excellent assistance in the preparation of the manuscript deserve special mention. Beth Heisey provided superb, extended help in the preparation of the first draft. LeRoy Burger and Kathy Whittle gave excellent assistance in the revisions.

Without Beth Heisey's superb work over many months as assistant editor, this project would have been impossible. Also crucial were Leroy Burger's help with the introductions and Kathy Whittle's typing. To the large number of scholars whose valuable criticism helped eliminate some of the problems and .mistakes in the first version, I can only say a profound thank you.

All Scripture quotations in this publication are from the Today's English Version Bible-Old Testament: Copyright © American Bible Society 1976, New Testament: Copyright © American Bible Society 1966, 1971, 1976. Used by permission.

Library of Congress
Catalog Card Number: 80-82133

Paulist Press ISBN: 0–8091–2308–8
and
InterVarsity Press ISBN: 0-87784-495X

Published by Paulist Press
Editorial Office: 1865 Broadway, New York, N.Y. 10023
Business Office: 545 Island Road, Ramsey, N.J. 07446
and
InterVarsity Press
Downers Grove, Illinois 60515

Printed and Bound in the United States of America

CONTENTS

INTRODUCTION

The Bible is an invitation to joy and celebration. It is also an invitation to forgiveness and grace. In fact the first flows from the second. The one who meets us in Holy Scripture assures us that he loves us just as we are in spite of our weakness, failure and sin. Therefore we celebrate the salvation, so freely offered by God, with joyful abandon.

But the Bible is also an invitation to repentance and change. The one who discloses himself as boundless love also reveals himself as truth, holiness and justice. Therefore he calls those to whom he freely offers his grace to repent, forsake their self-centered ways and begin to love their neighbors as themselves.

Love for God is inseparable from love for neighbor. Nor is that an abstract theoretical truth. If Jesus is right that anyone in need is our neighbor, then it has concrete, challenging implications in every historical context. In fact it can only be truly understood and faithfully applied as one looks honestly and courageously at one's particular situation in history.

Who are the needy neighbors that God invites us to love and serve today? Certainly they are people of all races, classes, continents, sexes and ages. But none of our neighbors face more desperate need than those who are so poor that malnutrition and even death constantly haunt them.

In 1977, the National Academy of Sciences published a study which pointed out that "750 million people in the poorest nations live in extreme poverty with annual incomes of less than $75." Hundreds of millions more in middle-income developing countries also subsist at poverty level incomes.[1] In 1974, the United Nations' *Development Forum* reported that "at least 462 million are actually starving," and recent United Nations reports indicate that there has been little change in the last four years. In addition, there are many more who have a minimally adequate calorie intake but lack sufficient protein. At least one half billion and probably as many as one billion persons in our world today are starving and/or malnourished.

How does our situation compare with theirs? After years of careful comparison of total output and real purchasing power around the world, Professor Irving Kravis of the University of Pennsylvania concluded that the average U.S. citizen is fourteen times as rich as the average Indian, seventeen times as rich as the average Kenyan. The average person in the U.S. consumes five times as much grain as the average person in Asia.

And still we think we are poor. In its September 12, 1977 issue, *Newsweek* did a major story on "The Middle Class Poor." Millions of North Americans actually believe that they can barely survive on the $15,000, $18,000 or even $25,000 they earn each year.

> Millions of American families who have earned their way to a middle-class income ... now find themselves struggling to make ends meet on salaries of $15,000 to $20,000 or more. ... According to a recent Gallup poll, more than half of all American families believe that balancing the family budget is their No. 1 problem. ... "We're not poor enough to go on welfare, but not rich enough to write a check to the plumber," says a Chicago secretary who works to supplement her husband's $23,000 salary as an accountant.

If the 750 million persons with less than $75 per year were to read this story (they will not, of course, because they are illiterate and the magazine would cost them a week's supply of food), they would be astonished.

That is the context in which we live. That is the context in which the God of love and justice invites us to love our needy neighbors out of gratitude for the way he loves us. We need to remember Karl Barth's call for Christians to take the Bible in one hand and the newspaper in the other. Careful study of the biblical teaching on the poor, possessions and justice, combined with sophisticated analysis of contemporary poverty and its systemic causes, is a criterion of a faithful Church in an age of hunger.

This collection of biblical passages is designed to assist in that study. The first brief section invites the reader to reflect on God's gracious gift of salvation as the source of grateful service to neighbor. Section II explores the character and extent of God's concern for the poor. Section III looks into the nature of the redeemed economic relationships God desires for his people. The extent and character of the Bible's concern for questions of property and possessions explained in section IV may surprise Western Christians. Section V enables the reader to reflect on God's concern for justice. The final brief section presents the biblical invitation to faithful stewardship and costly discipleship.

This collection of texts could have been arranged in many different ways. A more systematic, theological analysis of the biblical material in terms of the categories used here is perhaps only one way to support this particular arrangement. Those interested in my own attempt to do that are referred to chapters 3–6 of *Rich Christians in an Age of Hunger: A Biblical Study* (Inter-Varsity and Paulist, 1977).

The sheer volume of biblical material that pertains to questions of hunger, justice and the poor is astonishing. Hopefully this collection, which brings all these texts together in one place, will help the contemporary Church to understand this biblical truth more clearly.

But it dare not be seen as a canon within the canon. This collection of texts is *not* a collection of the most important or the most relevant biblical material for the late

3

twentieth century. It is merely a collection of biblical material on one particular cluster of issues. To view these texts as the most central within the Bible would be to distort both the editor's intentions and also the contemporary mission of the Church. On the other hand, simply to feel and experience the power, volume and frequency of what the Bible says about poverty, justice and hunger forcefully affects one's thought and life. I have been studying biblical teaching on these themes for years. But the task of bringing all of this biblical material together reminded me in a new, forceful way that the God disclosed in Scripture has a very deep concern for the poor, hungry and oppressed.

It is also necessary to insist that this collection of biblical texts is not a substitute for careful historical scholarship. To understand any biblical passage fully, one needs a vast amount of knowledge about many things, including the oral and/or literary history of the text and the historical setting of the author. Building on this detailed exegetical work, biblical theology weaves together the vast array of material from diverse historical periods and literary strands into a more unified synthesis. Both tasks are difficult and complex. Both tasks have produced considerable disagreement in the Church today. This collection did not seem to be the place to try to solve complex disputes of critical biblical scholarship. In the preparation of this reader, it has been my intention to profit from the wealth of material produced by modern biblical scholars. At the same time, it did not seem appropriate for the purposes of this study to adopt the approach of any particular scholar or school of interpretation.

A wide range of Protestant and Catholic commentaries have been consulted in the preparation of this collection. The reader is strongly urged to use a good contemporary commentary.[2]

Finally, this collection in no way pretends to solve complex hermeneutical issues. This reader places side by side texts from diverse historical periods and literary genres. It places wisdom literature alongside prophetic invective, ancient Israelite legal traditions alongside the Gospels and Paul. Obviously there are many valid ways to approach and organize the biblical material. Some are most helpful to illustrate one point, some to make another. The approach taken here reflects a conscious attempt to underline the cumulative impact of the fact that all strands of biblical literature display major concern for the poor, hungry and oppressed even though diverse strands emerged in very different historical settings over the course of two millennia of history.

The historical setting in first-century Palestine differed greatly from the historical context of Moses' time. And both differ even more from our global village in the late twentieth century. It is not an easy task to apply biblical texts from diverse literary strands and historical periods to the life and thought of the contemporary Church. In spite of hermeneutical complexities, however, Christians persist in their belief that this can be done. This collection and the accompanying study guide assume that the entire biblical canon still speaks to the Church today. But it does not assume any particular hermeneutic on the part of the reader. Each person will operate with different principles of interpretation. Some will use a complex hermeneutic, others a more simple one. But the one that chose to use the Scriptures as an instrument of revelation surely is able to speak to all.

This collection of biblical material is an invitation to hear God speak today. That his word may be startling, even disturbing, should not surprise us. Throughout history, God's word has constantly challenged as well as comforted. But the one who calls us to rethink our relationship to a billion hungry neighbors is the one whose love for us was so boundless that it took his Son to the cross. Thus the invitation to hear his word again today is not only a call to costly discipleship. It is also an invitation to joy and salvation.

NOTES

1. *World Food and Nutrition Study: The Potential Contributions of Research* (Washington: National Academy of Sciences, 1977), p. 34.

2. The following are widely used today: William Foxwell Albright and David Noel Freedman, editors, *The Anchor Bible* (Garden City: Doubleday & Co., Inc., 1964–   ); Clifton J. Allen, editor, *The Broadman Bible Commentary* (Nashville: Broadman Press, c. 1969–1972); Charles A. Briggs, S. R. Driver, and Alfred Plummer, editors, *The International Critical Commentary on the Holy Scriptures of the Old and New Testaments* (New York: Charles Scribner's Sons, 1895–   ); Raymond E. Brown, Joseph A. Fitzmeyer and Roland E. Murphy, editors, *The Jerome Biblical Commentary* (2 vols.; Englewood Cliffs, N.J.: Prentice-Hall, 1968); George Arthur Buttrick, *et al.*, editors, *The Interpreter's Bible* (New York: Abingdon Cokesbury, c. 1951–1956); Reginald C. Fuller, editor, *A New Catholic Commentary on Holy Scripture* (London: Nelson, 1969); D. Guthrie and J. A. Motyer, editors, *The New Bible Commentary* (revised edition; London: Inter-Varsity Press, 1970); R. V. G. Tasker, editor, *The Tyndale New Testament Commentaries* (Grand Rapids: Eerdmans, 1957–); D. J. Wiseman, editor, *The Tyndale Old Testament Commentaries* (Chicago: Inter-Varsity Press, 1964–   ).

ABBREVIATIONS

BB   Allen, Clifton J., editor. *The Broadman Bible Commentary.* Nashville: Broadman Press, c. 1969–1972.

IB   Buttrick, George Arthur, *et al.*, editors. *The Interpreter's Bible.* New York: Abingdon Cokesbury, c. 1951–1956.

ICC   Briggs, Charles A., S. R. Driver, and Alfred Plummer, editors. *The International Critical Commentary on the Holy Scriptures of the Old and New Testaments.* New York: Charles Scribner's Sons, 1895– .

JBC   Brown, Raymond E., *et al.*, editors. *The Jerome Biblical Commentary.* 2 vols. Englewood Cliffs, N.J.: Prentice-Hall, 1968.

NBC   Guthrie, D. and J. A. Motyer, editors. *The New Bible Commentary,* revised edition. London: Inter-Varsity Press, 1970.

NCC   Fuller, Reginald C., editor. *A New Catholic Commentary on Holy Scripture.* London: Nelson, 1969.

TNT   Tasker, R. V. G., editor. *The Tyndale New Testament Commentaries.* Grand Rapids: Eerdmans, 1957– .

TOT   Wiseman, D. J., editor, *The Tyndale Old Testament Commentaries.* Chicago: Inter-Varsity Press, 1964–.

I

SALVATION, SERVICE AND ULTIMATE SHALOM

SALVATION, SERVICE AND ULTIMATE SHALOM

Saved Through Faith

EPHESIANS 2:8–10

8-9 For it is by God's grace that you have been saved through faith. It is not the result of your own efforts, but God's gift, so that no one can boast about it. 10God has made us what we are, and in our union with Christ Jesus he has created us for a life of good deeds, which he has already prepared for us to do.

A GOOD CREATION CORRUPTED

The Story of Creation

GENESIS 1:1–31

In the beginning, when God created the universe,[a] 2 the earth was formless and desolate. The raging ocean that covered everything was engulfed in total darkness, and the power of God[b] was moving over the water. 3 Then God commanded, "Let there be light"—and light appeared. 4 God was pleased with what he saw. Then he separated the light from the darkness, 5 and he named the light "Day" and the darkness "Night." Evening passed and morning came—that was the first day.

6-7 Then God commanded, "Let there be a dome to divide the water and to keep it in two separate places"— and it was done. So God made a dome, and it separated the water under it from the water above it. 8 He named the dome "Sky." Evening passed and morning came—that was the second day.

⁹ Then God commanded, "Let the water below the sky come together in one place, so that the land will appear"—and it was done. ¹⁰ He named the land "Earth," and the water which had come together he named "Sea."ᵇ And God was pleased with what he saw. ¹¹ Then he commanded, "Let the earth produce all kinds of plants, those that bear grain and those that bear fruit"—and it was done. ¹² So the earth produced all kinds of plants, and God was pleased with what he saw. ¹³ Evening passed and morning came—that was the third day.

¹⁴ Then God commanded, "Let lights appear in the sky to separate day from night and to show the time when days, year, and religious festivalsᶜ begin; ¹⁵ they will shine in the sky to give light to the earth"—and it was done. ¹⁶ So God made the two larger lights, the sun to rule over the day and the moon to rule over the night; he also made the stars. ¹⁷ He placed the lights in the sky to shine on the earth, ¹⁸ to rule over the day and the night, and to separate light from darkness. And God was pleased with what he saw. ¹⁹ Evening passed and morning came—that was the fourth day.

²⁰ Then God commanded, "Let the water be filled with many kinds of living beings, and let the air be filled with birds." ²¹ So God created the great sea monsters, all kinds of creatures that live in the water, and all kinds of birds. And God was pleased with what he saw. ²² He blessed them all and told the creatures that live in the water to reproduce and to fill the sea, and he told the birds to increase in number. ²³ Evening passed and morning came—that was the fifth day.

²⁴ Then God commanded, "Let the earth produce all kinds of animal life: domestic and wild, large and small"—and it was done. ²⁵ So God made them all, and he was pleased with what he saw.

²⁶ Then God said, "And now we will make human beings; they will be like us and resemble us. They will

have power over the fish, the birds, and all animals, domestic and wild,[d] large and small." [27] So God created human beings, making them to be like himself. He created them male and female, [28] blessed them, and said, "Have many children, so that your descendants will live all over the earth and bring it under their control. I am putting you in charge of the fish, the birds, and all the wild animals. [29] I have provided all kinds of grain and all kinds of fruit for you to eat; [30] but for all the wild animals and for all the birds I have provided grass and leafy plants for food"—and it was done. [31] God looked at everything he had made, and he was very pleased. Evening passed and morning came—that was the sixth day.

The Guilt of Mankind

ROMANS 1:18–25
[18] God's anger is revealed from heaven against all the sin and evil of the people whose evil ways prevent the truth from being known. [19] God punishes them, because what can be known about God is plain. [20] Ever since God created the world, his invisible qualities, both his eternal power and his divine nature, have been clearly seen; they are perceived in the things that God has made. So those people have no excuse at all! [21] They know God, but they do not give him the honor that belongs to him, nor do they thank him. Instead, their thoughts have become complete nonsense, and their empty minds are filled with darkness. [22] They say they are wise, but they are fools; [23] instead of worshiping the immortal God, they worship images made to look like mortal man or birds or animals or reptiles.

[24] And so God has given those people over to do the filthy things their hearts desire, and they do shameful things with each other. [25] They exchange the truth about God for a lie; they worship and serve what God has created instead of the Creator himself, who is to be praised forever! Amen.

No One Is Righteous

ROMANS 3:9–18

⁹ Well then, are we Jews in any better condition than the Gentiles? Not at all!ᶜ I have already shown that Jews and Gentiles alike are all under the power of sin. ¹⁰ As the Scriptures say:

"There is no one who is righteous,
¹¹ no one who is wise
or who worships God.
¹² All have turned away from God;
they have all gone wrong;
no one does what is right, not even one.
¹³ Their words are full of deadly deceit;
wicked lies roll off their tongues,
and dangerous threats, like snake's poison, from their
lips;
¹⁴ their speech is filled with bitter curses.
¹⁵ They are quick to hurt and kill;
¹⁶ they leave ruin and destruction wherever they go.
¹⁷ They have not known the path of peace,
¹⁸ nor have they learned reverence for God."

GOD'S LOVE FOR SINNERS

No God Like You

MICAH 7:18–20

¹⁸ There is no other god like you, O LORD; you forgive the sins of your people who have survived. You do not stay angry forever, but you take pleasure in showing us your constant love. ¹⁹ You will be merciful to us once again. You will trample our sins underfoot and send them to the bottom of the sea! ²⁰ You will show your faithfulness and constant love to your people, the descen-

dants of Abraham and of Jacob, as you promised our ancestors long ago.

Christ Died for Us

ROMANS 5:6–11

⁶ For when we were still helpless, Christ died for the wicked at the time that God chose. ⁷ It is a difficult thing for someone to die for a righteous person. It may even be that someone might dare to die for a good person. ⁸ But God has shown us how much he loves us—it was while we were still sinners that Christ died for us! ⁹ By his death we are now put right with God; how much more, then, will we be saved by him from God's anger! ¹⁰ We were God's enemies, but he made us his friends through the death of his Son. Now that we are God's friends, how much more will we be saved by Christ's life! ¹¹ But that is not all; we rejoice because of what God has done through our Lord Jesus Christ, who has now made us God's friends.

His Only Son

JOHN 3:16–21

¹⁶ For God loved the world so much that he gave his only Son, so that everyone who believes in him may not die but have eternal life. ¹⁷ For God did not send his Son into the world to be its judge, but to be its savior.

¹⁸ Whoever believes in the Son is not judged; but whoever does not believe has already been judged, because he has not believed in God's only Son. ¹⁹ This is how the judgment works: the light has come into the world, but people love the darkness rather than the light, because their deeds are evil. ²⁰ Anyone who does evil things hates the light and will not come to the light, because he does not want his evil deeds to be shown up. ²¹ But whoever does what is true comes to the light in or-

der that the light may show that what he did was in obedience to God.

SALVATION BY GRACE

God's Offer of Mercy

ISAIAH 55:1
    The LORD says,
"Come, everyone who is thirsty—
  here is water!
Come, you that have no money—
  buy grain and eat!
Come! Buy wine and milk—
  it will cost you nothing!

Right with God

ROMANS 3:19–26
¹⁹ Now we know that everything in the Law applies to those who live under the Law, in order to stop all human excuses and bring the whole world under God's judgment. ²⁰ For no one is put right in God's sight by doing what the Law requires; what the Law does is to make man know that he has sinned.

²¹ But now God's way of putting people right with himself has been revealed. It has nothing to do with law, even though the Law of Moses and the prophets gave their witness to it. ²² God puts people right through their faith in Jesus Christ. God does this to all who believe in Christ, because there is no difference at all: ²³ everyone has sinned and is far away from God's saving presence. ²⁴ But by the free gift of God's grace all are put right with him through Christ Jesus, who sets them free. ²⁵⁻²⁶ God

offered him, so that by his death he should become the means by which people's sins are forgiven through their faith in him. God did this in order to demonstrate that he is righteous. In the past he was patient and overlooked people's sins; but in the present time he deals with their sins, in order to demonstrate his righteousness. In this way God shows that he himself is righteous and that he puts right everyone who believes in Jesus.

ROMANS 5:1–5

Now that we have been put right with God through faith, we have[d] peace with God through our Lord Jesus Christ. ² He has brought us by faith into this experience of God's grace, in which we now live. And so we boast[e] of the hope we have of sharing God's glory! ³ We also boast[f] of our troubles, because we know that trouble produces endurance, ⁴ endurance brings God's approval, and his approval creates hope. ⁵ This hope does not disappoint us, for God has poured out his love into our hearts by means of the Holy Spirit, who is God's gift to us.

Dead to Sin but Alive in Christ

ROMANS 6:1–14

What shall we say, then? Should we continue to live in sin so that God's grace will increase? ² Certainly not! We have died to sin—how then can we go on living in it? ³ For surely you know that when we were baptized into union with Christ Jesus, we were baptized into union with his death. ⁴ By our baptism, then, we were buried with him and shared his death, in order that, just as Christ was raised from death by the glorious power of the Father, so also we might live a new life.

⁵ For since we have become one with him in dying as he did, in the same way we shall be one with him by being raised to life as he was. ⁶ And we know that our old being has been put to death with Christ on his cross, in order that the power of the sinful self might be destroyed,

16

so that we should no longer be the slaves of sin. [7] For when a person dies, he is set free from the power of sin. [8] Since we have died with Christ, we believe that we will also live with him. [9] For we know that Christ has been raised from death and will never die again—death will no longer rule over him. [10] And so, because he died, sin has no power over him; and now he lives his life in fellowship with God. [11] In the same way you are to think of yourselves as dead, so far as sin is concerned, but living in fellowship with God through Christ Jesus.

[12] Sin must no longer rule in your mortal bodies, so that you obey the desires of your natural self. [13] Nor must you surrender any part of yourselves to sin to be used for wicked purposes. Instead, give yourselves to God, as those who have been brought from death to life, and surrender your whole being to him to be used for righteous purposes. [14] Sin must not be your master; for you do not live under law but under God's grace.

Jesus the Bread of Life

JOHN 6:25–59

[25] When the people found Jesus on the other side of the lake, they said to him, "Teacher, when did you get here?"

[26] Jesus answered, "I am telling you the truth: you are looking for me because you ate the bread and had all you wanted, not because you understood my miracles. [27] Do not work for food that spoils; instead, work for the food that lasts for eternal life. This is the food which the Son of Man will give you, because God, the Father, has put his mark of approval on him."

[28] So they asked him, "What can we do in order to do what God wants us to do?"

[29] Jesus answered, "What God wants you to do is to believe in the one he sent."

[30] They replied, "What miracle will you perform so that we may see it and believe you? What will you do?

17

[31] Our ancestors ate manna in the desert, just as the scripture says, 'He gave them bread from heaven to eat.' "

[32] "I am telling you the truth," Jesus said. "What Moses gave you was not[m] the bread from heaven; it is my Father who gives you the real bread from heaven. [33] For the bread that God gives is he who comes down from heaven and gives life to the world."

[34] "Sir," they asked him, "give us this bread always."

[35] "I am the bread of life," Jesus told them. "He who comes to me will never be hungry; he who believes in me will never be thirsty. [36] Now, I told you that you have seen me but will not believe. [37] Everyone whom my Father gives me will come to me. I will never turn away anyone who comes to me, [38] because I have come down from heaven to do not my own will but the will of him who sent me. [39] And it is the will of him who sent me that I should not lose any of all those he has given me, but that I should raise them all to life on the last day. [40] For what my Father wants is that all who see the Son and believe in him should have eternal life. And I will raise them to life on the last day."

[41] The people started grumbling about him, because he said, "I am the bread that came down from heaven." [42] So they said, "This man is Jesus son of Joseph, isn't he? We know his father and mother. How, then, does he now say he came down from heaven?"

[43] Jesus answered, "Stop grumbling among yourselves. [44] No one can come to me unless the Father who sent me draws him to me; and I will raise him to life on the last day. [45] The prophets wrote, 'Everyone will be taught by God.' Anyone who hears the Father and learns from him comes to me. [46] This does not mean that anyone has seen the Father; he who is from God is the only one who has seen the Father. [47] I am telling you the truth: he who believes has eternal life. [48] I am the bread of life. [49] Your ancestors ate manna in the desert, but they died. [50] But the bread that comes down from heaven is of such a kind that whoever eats it will not die. [51] I am the living

18

bread that came down from heaven. If anyone eats this bread, he will live forever. The bread that I will give him is my flesh, which I give so that the world may live."

[52] This started an angry argument among them. "How can this man give us his flesh to eat?" they asked.

[53] Jesus said to them, "I am telling you the truth: if you do not eat the flesh of the Son of Man and drink his blood, you will not have life in yourselves. [54] Whoever eats my flesh and drinks my blood has eternal life, and I will raise him to life on the last day. [55] For my flesh is the real food; my blood is the real drink. [56] Whoever eats my flesh and drinks my blood lives in me, and I live in him. [57] The living Father sent me, and because of him I live also. In the same way whoever eats me will live because of me. [58] This, then, is the bread that came down from heaven; it is not like the bread that your ancestors ate, but then later died. The one who eats this bread will live forever."

[59] Jesus said this as he taught in the synagogue in Capernaum.

Saved by Grace

EPHESIANS 2:8–10

[8-9] For it is by God's grace that you have been saved through faith. It is not the result of your own efforts, but God's gift, so that no one can boast about it. [10] God has made us what we are, and in our union with Christ Jesus he has created us for a life of good deeds, which he has already prepared for us to do.

SERVING OTHERS OUT OF JOYFUL GRATITUDE

Love One Another

1 JOHN 3:11–18

¹¹ The message you heard from the very beginning is this: we must love one another. ¹² We must not be like Cain; he belonged to the Evil One and murdered his own brother Abel. Why did Cain murder him? Because the things he himself did were wrong, and the things his brother did were right.

¹³ So do not be surprised, my brothers, if the people of the world hate you. ¹⁴ We know that we have left death and come over into life; we know it because we love our brothers. Whoever does not love is still under the power of death. ¹⁵ Whoever hates his brother is a murderer, and you know that a murderer does not have eternal life in him. ¹⁶ This is how we know what love is: Christ gave his life for us. We too, then, ought to give our lives for our brothers! ¹⁷ If a rich person sees his brother in need, yet closes his heart against his brother, how can he claim that he loves God? ¹⁸ My children, our love should not be just words and talk; it must be true love, which shows itself in action.

DEUTERONOMY 24:17–18

¹⁷ "Do not deprive foreigners and orphans of their rights; and do not take a widow's garment as security for a loan. ¹⁸ Remember that you were slaves in Egypt and that the LORD your God set you free; that is why I have given you this command.

Because He Loved Us

1 JOHN 4:7–12

7 Dear friends, let us love one another, because love comes from God. Whoever loves is a child of God and knows God. 8 Whoever does not love does not know God, for God is love. 9 And God showed his love for us by sending his only Son into the world, so that we might have life through him. 10 This is what love is: it is not that we have loved God, but that he loved us and sent his Son to be the means by which our sins are forgiven.

11 Dear friends, if this is how God loved us, then we should love one another. 12 No one has ever seen God, but if we love one another, God lives in union with us, and his love is made perfect in us.

Broken for Us

1 CORINTHIANS 11:23–26

23 For I received from the Lord the teaching that I passed on to you: that the Lord Jesus, on the night he was betrayed, took a piece of bread, 24 gave thanks to God, broke it, and said, "This is my body, which is for you. Do this in memory of me." 25 In the same way, after the supper he took the cup and said, "This cup is God's new covenant, sealed with my blood. Whenever you drink it, do so in memory of me."

26 This means that every time you eat this bread and drink from this cup you proclaim the Lord's death until he comes.

Righteousness Through Faith

PHILIPPIANS 3:3–11

3 It is we, not they, who have received the true circumcision, for we worship God by means of his Spirit and rejoice in our life in union with Christ Jesus. We do not put any trust in external ceremonies. 4 I could, of

course, put my trust in such things. If anyone thinks he can trust in external ceremonies, I have even more reason to feel that way. [5] I was circumcised when I was a week old. I am an Israelite by birth, of the tribe of Benjamin, a pure-blooded Hebrew. As far as keeping the Jewish Law is concerned, I was a Pharisee, [6] and I was so zealous that I persecuted the church. As far as a person can be righteous by obeying the commands of the Law, I was without fault. [7] But all those things that I might count as profit I now reckon as loss for Christ's sake. [8] Not only those things; I reckon everything as complete loss for the sake of what is so much more valuable, the knowledge of Christ Jesus my Lord. For his sake I have thrown everything away; I consider it all as mere garbage, so that I may gain Christ [9] and be completely united with him. I no longer have a righteousness of my own, the kind that is gained by obeying the Law. I now have the righteousness that is given through faith in Christ, the righteousness that comes from God and is based on faith. [10] All I want is to know Christ and to experience the power of his resurrection, to share in his sufferings and become like him in his death, [11] in the hope that I myself will be raised from death to life.

Giving as Christ Gave

2 CORINTHIANS 8:1–9

Our brothers, we want you to know what God's grace has accomplished in the churches in Macedonia. [2] They have been severely tested by the troubles they went through; but their joy was so great that they were extremely generous in their giving, even though they are very poor. [3] I can assure you that they gave as much as they could, and even more than they could. Of their own free will [4] they begged us and pleaded for the privilege of having a part in helping God's people in Judea. [5] It was more than we could have hoped for! First they gave themselves to the Lord; and then, by God's will they gave themselves to us as well. [6] So we urged Titus, who began this work, to continue it and help you complete this special service of love. [7] You are so rich in all you have: in faith, speech, and knowledge, in your eagerness to help and in your love for us.[c] And so we want you to be generous also in this service of love.

[8] I am not laying down any rules. But by showing how eager others are to help, I am trying to find out how real your own love is. [9] You know the grace of our Lord Jesus Christ; rich as he was, he made himself poor for your sake, in order to make you rich by means of his poverty.

SALVATION COMPLETED: THE SHALOM

FOR WHICH WE HOPE

The Lord's Universal Reign of Peace

MICAH 4:1–4

In days to come
the mountain where the Temple stands
   will be the highest one of all,
   towering above all the hills.
Many nations will come streaming to it,
2   and their people will say,
"Let us go up the hill of the LORD,
   to the Temple of Israel's God.
For he will teach us what he wants us to do;
   we will walk in the paths he has chosen.
For the LORD's teaching comes from Jerusalem;
   from Zion he speaks to his people."
3 He will settle disputes among the nations,
   among the great powers near and far.

They will hammer their swords into plows
   and their spears into pruning knives.
Nations will never again go to war,
   never prepare for battle again.
⁴ Everyone will live in peace
   among his own vineyards and fig trees,
   and no one will make him afraid.
The LORD Almighty has promised this.

When the Mortal Becomes Immortal

1 CORINTHIANS 15:3–8; 20–26; 51–58

³ I passed on to you what I received, which is of the greatest importance: that Christ died for our sins, as written in the Scriptures; ⁴ that he was buried and that he was raised to life three days later, as written in the Scriptures; ⁵ that he appeared to Peter and then to all twelve apostles. ⁶ Then he appeared to more than five hundred of his followers at once, most of whom are still alive, although some have died. ⁷ Then he appeared to James, and afterward to all the apostles.

⁸ Last of all he appeared also to me—even though I am like someone whose birth was abnormal.ᵒ

²⁰ But the truth is that Christ has been raised from death, as the guarantee that those who sleep in death will also be raised. ²¹ For just as death came by means of a man, in the same way the rising from death comes by means of a man. ²² For just as all people die because of their union with Adam, in the same way all will be raised to life because of their union with Christ. ²³ But each one will be raised in his proper order: Christ, first of all; then, at the time of his coming, those who belong to him. ²⁴ Then the end will come; Christ will overcome all spiritual rulers, authorities, and powers, and will hand over the Kingdom to God the Father. ²⁵ For Christ must rule until God defeats all enemies and puts them under his feet. ²⁶ The last enemy to be defeated will be death.

⁵¹⁻⁵² Listen to this secret truth: we shall not all die,

but when the last trumpet sounds, we shall all be changed in an instant, as quickly as the blinking of an eye. For when the trumpet sounds, the dead will be raised, never to die again, and we shall all be changed. [53] For what is mortal must be changed into what is immortal; what will die must be changed into what cannot die. [54] So when this takes place, and the mortal has been changed into the immortal, then the scripture will come true: "Death is destroyed; victory is complete!"

[55] "Where, Death, is your victory?
        Where, Death, is your power to hurt?"

[56] Death gets its power to hurt from sin, and sin gets its power from the Law. [57] But thanks be to God who gives us the victory through our Lord Jesus Christ!

[58] So then, my dear brothers, stand firm and steady. Keep busy always in your work for the Lord, since you know that nothing you do in the Lord's service is ever useless.

The Future Glory

ROMANS 8:18–25

[18] I consider that what we suffer at this present time cannot be compared at all with the glory that is going to be revealed to us. [19] All of creation waits with eager longing for God to reveal his sons. [20] For creation was condemned to lose its purpose, not of its own will, but because God willed it to be so. Yet there was the hope [21] that creation itself would one day be set free from its slavery to decay and would share the glorious freedom of the children of God. [22] For we know that up to the present time all of creation groans with pain, like the pain of childbirth. [23] But it is not just creation alone which groans; we who have the Spirit as the first of God's gifts also groan within ourselves as we wait for God to make us his sons and set our whole being free. [24] For it was by hope that we were saved; but if we see what we hope for, then it is not really hope. For who hopes for something

he sees! [25] But if we hope for what we do not see, we wait for it with patience.

The New Heaven and the New Earth

REVELATION 21:1–6

Then I saw a new heaven and a new earth. The first heaven and the first earth disappeared, and the sea vanished. [2] And I saw the Holy City, the new Jerusalem, coming down out of heaven from God, prepared and ready, like a bride dressed to meet her husband. [3] I heard a loud voice speaking from the throne: "Now God's home is with mankind! He will live with them, and they shall be his people. God himself will be with them, and he will be their God. [4] He will wipe away all tears from their eyes. There will be no more death, no more grief or crying or pain. The old things have disappeared."

[5] Then the one who sits on the throne said, "And now I make all things new!" He also said to me, "Write this, because these words are true and can be trusted." [6] And he said, "It is done! I am the first and the last, the beginning and the end. To anyone who is thirsty I will give the right to drink from the spring of the water of life without paying for it.

II

GOD'S SPECIAL CONCERN
FOR THE POOR

PIVOTAL POINTS OF REVELATION
HISTORY

Rights of the Oppressed

PSALM 103:6–7

⁶ The LORD judges in favor of the oppressed
   and gives them their rights.
⁷ He revealed his plans to Moses
   and let the people of Israel see his mighty deeds.

EXODUS

Punishing the Nation That Enslaves Them

GENESIS 15:12–14

¹² When the sun was going down, Abram fell into a
deep sleep, and fear and terror came over him. ¹³ The
LORD said to him, "Your descendants will be strangers in
a foreign land; they will be slaves there and will be treated cruelly for four hundred years. ¹⁴ But I will punish the
nation that enslaves them, and when they leave that foreign land, they will take great wealth with them.

Exile in Egypt

EXODUS 3:7–10

⁷ Then the LORD said, "I have seen how cruelly my
people are being treated in Egypt; I have heard them cry
out to be rescued from their slave drivers. I know all
about their sufferings, ⁸ and so I have come down to rescue them from the Egyptians and to bring them out of
Egypt to a fertile and spacious land, one which is rich

and fertile and in which the Canaanites, the Hittites, the Amorites, the Perizzites, the Hivites, and the Jebusites now live. ⁹ I have indeed heard the cry of my people, and I see how the Egyptians are oppressing them. ¹⁰ Now I am sending you to the king of Egypt so that you can lead my people out of his country."

EXODUS 6:2–9

² God spoke to Moses and said, "I am the LORD. ³ I appeared to Abraham, to Isaac, and to Jacob as Almighty God, but I did not make myself known to them by my holy name, the LORD.ᵍ ⁴ I also made my covenant with them, promising to give them the land of Canaan, the land in which they had lived as foreigners. ⁵ Now I have heard the groaning of the Israelites, whom the Egyptians have enslaved, and I have remembered my covenant. ⁶ So tell the Israelites that I say to them, 'I am the LORD; I will rescue you and set you free from your slavery to the Egyptians. I will raise my mighty arm to bring terrible punishment upon them, and I will save you. ⁷ I will make you my own people, and I will be your God. You will know that I am the LORD your God when I set you free from slavery in Egypt. ⁸ I will bring you to the land that I solemnly promised to give to Abraham, Isaac, and Jacob; and I will give it to you as your own possession. I am the LORD.' " ⁸ Moses told this to the Israelites, but they would not listen to him, because their spirit had been broken by their cruel slavery.

God Saw the Suffering

DEUTERONOMY 26:1–11

"After you have occupied the land that the LORD your God is giving you and have settled there, ²each of you must place in a basket the first part of each crop that you harvest and you must take it with you to the one place of worship. ³ Go to the priest in charge at that time and say to him, 'I now acknowledge to the LORD my

God that I have entered the land that he promised our ancestors to give us.'

4 "The priest will take the basket from you and place it before the altar of the LORD your God. 5 Then, in the LORD's presence you will recite these words: 'My ancestor was a wandering Aramean, who took his family to Egypt to live. They were few in number when they went there, but they became a large and powerful nation. 6 The Egyptians treated us harshly and forced us to work as slaves. 7 Then we cried out for help to the LORD, the God of our ancestors. He heard us and saw our suffering, hardship, and misery. 8 By his great power and strength he rescued us from Egypt. He worked miracles and wonders, and caused terrifying things to happen. 9 He brought us here and gave us this rich and fertile land. 10 So now I bring to the LORD the first part of the harvest that he has given me.'

"Then set the basket down in the LORD's presence and worship there. 11 Be grateful for the good things that the LORD your God has given you and your family; and let the Levites and the foreigners who live among you join in the celebration.

DESTRUCTION OF ISRAEL AND JUDAH

If You Do Not Obey

JEREMIAH 22:1–5
1-2 The LORD told me to go to the palace of the king of Judah, the descendant of David, and there tell the king, his officials, and the people of Jerusalem to listen to what the LORD had said: 3 "I, the LORD, command you to do what is just and right. Protect the person who is being cheated from the one who is cheating him. Do not mistreat or oppress aliens, orphans, or widows; and do not kill innocent people in this holy place. 4 If you really do as I have commanded, then David's descendants will

continue to be kings. And they, together with their officials and their people, will continue to pass through the gates of this palace in chariots and on horses. ⁵ But if you do not obey my commands, then I swear to you that this palace will fall into ruins. I, the LORD, have spoken.

INTRODUCTION TO AMOS 4:1–3

Amos addressed a wealthy society. In the eighth century, Israel enjoyed a prosperity unknown since the days of Solomon. But the shocking contrast between the rich and the poor greatly disturbed Amos. He was furious that the powerful and wealthy had developed much of their wealth precisely through exploitation of the poor. When poorer land owners needed to borrow money, they could do so only at a very high interest rate. When they could not repay the loans, they lost their property. Although the ancient laws of Israel declared that the property could always be redeemed if the money owed was repaid, the legal institutions in Amos' day were controlled by corrupt officials whom the wealthy could easily bribe. Consequently, the rich became richer and the poor became poorer.

In this passage, Amos addresses his message to the rich women of Israel, comparing them to the great cattle of Bashan, a land to the north. There cattle, although rather stubborn, were of a very high quality and, as such, were highly prized. Similarly, the women of Samaria were spoiled and fattened at the expense of the poor. They encouraged their husbands to oppress the weak so that they could indulge in ever greater luxuries. The Lord swears that these women will be dragged away by a foreign enemy. The destruction will be so total that they will not need to look for the city gates, for they will be able to pass through the huge holes in the walls made by the foreign conqueror (v.3).

For further study: in addition to BB, IB, ICC, NBC, and NCC, see also S. R. Driver, Joel and Amos *("The Cambridge Bible," Cambridge: The University Press, 1942); James Luther Mays,* Amos *(Philadelphia: The*

Westminster Press, 1969); J. A. Motyer, The Day of the
Lion *(Downers Grove: Inter-Varsity Press, 1974).*

Women Who Oppress the Poor

AMOS 4:1–3

Listen to this, you women of Samaria, who grow fat
like the well-fed cows of Bashan, who mistreat the weak,
oppress the poor, and demand that your husbands keep
you supplied with liquor! [2] As the Sovereign LORD is
holy, he has promised, "The days will come when they
will drag you away with hooks; every one of you will be
like a fish on a hook. [3] You will be dragged to the nearest
break in the wall and thrown out."

The Wages of Sin

MICAH 2:1–10

How terrible it will be for those who lie awake and
plan evil! When morning comes, as soon as they have the
chance, they do the evil they planned. [2] When they want
fields, they seize them; when they want houses, they take
them. No man's family or property is safe.

[3] And so the LORD says, "I am planning to bring disaster on you, and you will not be able to escape it. You
are going to find yourselves in trouble, and then you will
not walk so proudly any more. [4] When that time comes,
people will use the story about you as an example of disaster, and they will sing this song of despair about your
experience:

We are completely ruined!
The LORD has taken our land away
And given it to those who took us captive."[b]

[5] So then, when the time comes for the land to be
given back to the LORD's people, there will be no share
for any of you.

⁶ The people preach at me and say, "Don't preach at us. Don't preach about all that. God is not going to disgrace us. ⁷ Do you think the people of Israel are under a curse?ᶜ Has the LORD lost his patience? Would he really do such things? Doesn't heᵈ speak kindly to those who do right?"

⁸ The LORD replies, "You attack my people like enemies. Men return from battle, thinking they are safe at home, but there you are, waiting to steal the coats off their backs.ᵉ ⁹ You drive the women of my people out of the homes they love, and you have robbed their children of my blessings forever. ¹⁰ Get up and go; there is no safety here any more. Your sins have doomed this place to destruction.

ZEPHANIAH **3:1**

Jerusalem is doomed, that corrupt, rebellious city that oppresses its own people.

Because They Would Not Listen

ZECHARIAH **7:8–14**

⁸ The LORD gave this message to Zechariah: ⁹ "Long ago I gave these commands to my people: 'You must see that justice is done, and must show kindness and mercy to one another.¹⁰ Do not oppress widows, orphans, foreigners who live among you, or anyone else in need. And do not plan ways of harming one another.'

¹¹ "But my people stubbornly refused to listen. They closed their minds ¹² and made their hearts as hard as rock. Because they would not listen to the teaching which I sent through the prophets who lived long ago, I became very angry. ¹³ Because they did not listen when I spoke, I did not answer when they prayed. ¹⁴ Like a storm I swept them away to live in foreign countries. This good land was left a desolate place, with no one living in it."

It was customary in the synagogues of Jesus' day for a portion of both the Law (the first five books of the Old Testament) and the prophets to be read. A section of the Law had probably already been read when Jesus stood up to read from the prophets. It was the custom for visiting rabbis to be given this opportunity.

The passage Jesus quotes is from Isaiah (61:1–2; 58:6), and it refers there to a person anointed by God to comfort the afflicted of Zion. Whether the passage Jesus read was a prescribed reading for the day, or whether it was a passage of Jesus' own choosing, has been much debated and is still not entirely certain. What is of course most significant here is Jesus' powerful application of it.

Some recent scholarship (e.g., Robert Sloan) believes that verse 19 refers to the Year of Jubilee (Lev. 25:8ff; see Lesson V). If this is correct and Jesus intended to announce the eschatological Jubilee here, then this passage indicates that significant socio-economic change was central to his mission. In any case, this text shows that concern for the poor, captive, and oppressed was important to him. That St. Luke places this programmatic passage at the beginning of Jesus' public ministry underlines its importance.

For further study: *in addition to BB, IB, ICC, NBC, and NCC, see also G. B. Caird,* The Gospel of St. Luke *("The Pelican Gospel Commentaries," Baltimore: Penguin Books, Inc., 1963); Hans Conzelmann,* The Theology of St. Luke, *trans. Geoffrey Buswell (New York: Harper and Row, 1960); Norval Geldenhuys,* Commentary on the Gospel of Luke *(Grand Rapids: Eerdmans, 1952); Leon Morris,* The Gospel According to St. Luke *(TNT, Grand Rapids: Eerdmans Pub. Co., 1974); Robert B. Sloan, Jr.,* The Favorable Year of the Lord: A Study of Jubilary Theology in the Gospel of Luke *(Ph.D. dissertation, Univ. of Basel; Austin, Texas: Schola Press, 1977).*

THE INCARNATION

Liberty to the Captives

LUKE 4:16–21

[16] Then Jesus went to Nazareth, where he had been brought up, and on the Sabbath he went as usual to the synagogue. He stood up to read the Scriptures [17] and was handed the book of the prophet Isaiah. He unrolled the scroll and found the place where it is written,

[18] "The Spirit of the Lord is upon me,
> because he has chosen me to bring good news to the poor.
> He has sent me to proclaim liberty to the captives
> and recovery of sight to the blind,
> to set free the oppressed
[19] and announce that the time has come
> when the Lord will save his people."

[20] Jesus rolled up the scroll, gave it back to the attendant, and sat down. All the people in the synagogue had their eyes fixed on him, [21] as he said to them, "This passage of scripture has come true today, as you heard it being read."

God's Servant and the Weak

MATTHEW 12:15–21

[15] When Jesus heard about the plot against him, he went away from that place; and large crowds followed him. He healed all the sick [16] and gave them orders not to tell others about him. [17] He did this so as to make come true what God had said through the prophet Isaiah:

[18] "Here is my servant, whom I have chosen,
> the one I love, and with whom I am pleased.

I will send my Spirit upon him,
> and he will announce my judgment to the nations.

¹⁹ He will not argue or shout,
> or make loud speeches in the streets.

²⁰ He will be gentle to those who are weak,
> and kind to those who are helpless.

He will persist until he causes justice to triumph,

²¹ and on him all peoples will put their hope."

Good News to the Poor

LUKE 7:18–23

¹⁸ When John's disciples told him about all these things, he called two of them ¹⁹ and sent them to the Lord to ask him, "Are you the one John said was going to come, or should we expect someone else?"

²⁰ When they came to Jesus, they said, "John the Baptist sent us to ask if you are the one he said was going to come, or should we expect someone else?"

²¹ At that very time Jesus healed many people from their sicknesses, diseases, and evil spirits, and gave sight to many blind people. ²² He answered John's messengers, "Go back and tell John what you have seen and heard: the blind can see, the lame can walk, those who suffer from dreaded skin diseases are made clean,ᶠ the deaf can hear, the dead are raised to life, and the Good News is preached to the poor. ²³ How happy are those who have no doubts about me!"

GOD'S SPECIAL IDENTIFICATION WITH
THE LEAST OF THESE

PROVERBS 19:17

¹⁷ When you give to the poor, it is like lending to the LORD, and the LORD will pay you back.

Special Sacrifices for the Poor

LEVITICUS 5:7–11

⁷ If a man cannot afford a sheep or a goat, he shall bring to the LORD as the payment for his sin two doves or two pigeons, one for a sin offering and the other for a burnt offering. ⁸ He shall bring them to the priest, who will first offer the bird for the sin offering. He will break its neck without pulling off its head ⁹ and sprinkle some of its blood against the side of the altar. The rest of the blood will be drained out at the base of the altar. This is an offering to take away sin. ¹⁰ Then he shall offer the second bird as a burnt offering, according to the regulations. In this way the priest shall offer the sacrifice for the man's sin, and he will be forgiven.

¹¹ If a man cannot afford two doves or two pigeons, he shall bring two pounds of flour as a sin offering.

LEVITICUS 12:6–8

⁶ When the time of her purification is completed, whether for a son or daughter, she shall bring to the priest at the entrance of the Tent of the LORD's presence a one-year-old lamb for a burnt offering and a pigeon or a dove for a sin offering. ⁷ The priest shall present her offering to the LORD and perform the ritual to take away her impurity, and she will be ritually clean. This, then, is what a woman must do after giving birth.

⁸ If the woman cannot afford a lamb, she shall bring

two doves or two pigeons, one for a burnt offering and the other for a sin offering, and the priest shall perform the ritual to take away her impurity, and she will be ritually clean.

LEVITICUS 14:1–22

The LORD gave Moses[2] the following regulations about the ritual purification of a person cured of a dreaded skin disease.

[10] On the eighth day he shall bring two male lambs and one female lamb a year old that are without any defects, five pounds of flour mixed with olive oil, and half a pint of olive oil.

[21] If the man is poor and cannot afford any more he shall bring for his purification only one male lamb as his repayment offering, a special gift to the LORD for the priest. He shall bring only two pounds of flour mixed with olive oil for a grain offering and half a pint of olive oil. [22] He shall also bring two doves or two pigeons, one for the sin offering and one for the burnt offering.

Protecting the Poor

PSALM 12:5

[5] "But now I will come," says the LORD,
    "because the needy are oppressed
    and the persecuted groan in pain.
I will give them the security they long for."

PSALM 35:10

[10] With all my heart I will say to the LORD,
    "There is no one like you.
    You protect the weak from the strong,
    the poor from the oppressor."

PSALM 68:5–6

[5] God, who lives in his sacred Temple,
    cares for orphans and protects widows.

⁶ He gives the lonely a home to live in
  and leads prisoners out into happy freedom,
  but rebels will have to live in a desolate land.

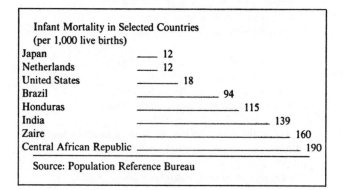

Infant Mortality in Selected Countries
(per 1,000 live births)

Japan	12
Netherlands	12
United States	18
Brazil	94
Honduras	115
India	139
Zaire	160
Central African Republic	190

Source: Population Reference Bureau

PSALM 69:30–33

³⁰ I will praise God with a song;
  I will proclaim his greatness by giving him thanks.
³¹ This will please the LORD more than offering him cattle,
  more than sacrificing a full-grown bull.
³² When the oppressed see this, they will be glad;
  those who worship God will be encouraged.
³³ The LORD listens to those in need
  and does not forget his people in prison.

PSALM 109:30–31

³⁰ I will give loud thanks to the LORD;
  I will praise him in the assembly of the people,
³¹ because he defends the poor man
  and saves him from those who condemn him to death.

PSALM 140:12

¹² LORD, I know that you defend the cause of the poor
  and the rights of the needy.

Creator and God of the Oppressed

PSALM 146:1–10

Praise the LORD!
 Praise the LORD, my soul!
2 I will praise him as long as I live;
 I will sing to my God all my life.

3 Don't put your trust in human leaders;
 no human being can save you.
4 When they die, they return to the dust;
 on that day all their plans come to an end.

5 Happy is the man who has the God of Jacob to help him
 and who depends on the LORD his God,

6 the Creator of heaven, earth, and sea,
 and all that is in them.
He always keeps his promises;
7 he judges in favor of the oppressed
 and gives food to the hungry.

The LORD sets prisoners free
8 and gives sight to the blind.
He lifts those who have fallen;
 he loves his righteous people.
9 He protects the strangers who live in our land;
 he helps widows and orphans,
 but ruins the plans of the wicked.

10 The LORD is king forever.
 Your God, O Zion, will reign for all time.

Praise the LORD!

Insulting God

PROVERBS 17:5

⁵ If you make fun of poor people, you insult the God who made them.

Hope for the Poor

ISAIAH 11:1–4

The royal line of David is like a tree that has been cut down; but just as new branches sprout from a stump, so a new king will arise from among David's descendants.

² The spirit of the LORD will give him wisdom
  and the knowledge and skill to rule his people.
He will know the LORD's will and will have reverence for
    him,
³ and find pleasure in obeying him.
  He will not judge by appearance or hearsay;
⁴ he will judge the poor fairly
  and defend the rights of the helpless.

ISAIAH 61:1

The Sovereign LORD has filled me with his spirit.
He has chosen me and sent me
To bring good news to the poor,
To heal the broken-hearted,
To announce release to captives
And freedom to those in prison.

The Poor with You

MARK 14:3–9

³ Jesus was in Bethany at the house of Simon, a man who had suffered from a dreaded skin disease. While Jesus was eating, a woman came in with an alabaster jar full of a very expensive perfume made of pure nard. She broke the jar and poured the perfume on Jesus' head.

⁴ Some of the people there became angry and said to one another, "What was the use of wasting the perfume? ⁵ It could have been sold for more than three hundred silver coins and the money given to the poor!" And they criticized her harshly.

⁶ But Jesus said, "Leave her alone! Why are you bothering her? She has done a fine and beautiful thing for me. ⁷ You will always have poor people with you, and any time you want to, you can help them. But you will not always have me. ⁸ She did what she could; she poured perfume on my body to prepare it ahead of time for burial. ⁹ Now, I assure you that wherever the gospel is preached all over the world, what she has done will be told in memory of her."

The Lost Sheep

LUKE 15:1–7

One day when many tax collectors and other outcasts came to listen to Jesus, ² the Pharisees and the teachers of the Law started grumbling, "This man welcomes outcasts and even eats with them!" ³ So Jesus told them this parable:

⁴ "Suppose one of you has a hundred sheep and loses one of them—what does he do? He leaves the other ninety-nine sheep in the pasture and goes looking for the one that got lost until he finds it. ⁵ When he finds it, he is so happy that he puts it on his shoulders ⁶ and carries it back home. Then he calls his friends and neighbors together and says to them, 'I am so happy I found my lost sheep. Let us celebrate!' ⁷ In the same way, I tell you, there will be more joy in heaven over one sinner who repents than over ninety-nine respectable people who do not need to repent.

LUKE 1:52–53

⁵² He has brought down mighty kings from their thrones,
      and lifted up the lowly.

⁵³ He has filled the hungry with good things,
and sent the rich away with empty hands.

Lifting the Poor from the Dust

1 SAMUEL 2:2–8

² "No one is holy like the LORD;
there is none like him,
no protector like our God.
³ Stop your loud boasting;
silence your proud words.
For the LORD is a God who knows,
and he judges all that people do.
⁴ The bows of strong soldiers are broken,
but the weak grow strong.
⁵ The people who once were well fed
now hire themselves out to get food,
but the hungry are hungry no more.
The childless wife has borne seven children,
but the mother of many is left with none.
⁶ The LORD kills and restores to life;
he sends people to the world of the dead
and brings them back again.
⁷ He makes some men poor and others rich;
he humbles some and makes others great.
⁸ He lifts the poor from the dust
and raises the needy from their misery.
He makes them companions of princes
and puts them in places of honor.
The foundations of the earth belong to the LORD;
on them he has built the world.

Saving the Needy from Oppression

JOB 5:11–16

¹¹ Yes, it is God who raises the humble
and gives joy to all who mourn.

¹² He upsets the plans of cunning men,
  and traps wise men in their own schemes,
¹³ so that nothing they do succeeds;
¹⁴ even at noon they grope in darkness.
¹⁵ But God saves the poor[k] from death,
  he saves the needy from oppression.
¹⁶ He gives hope to the poor and silences the wicked.

Always Ready To Help

PSALM 10:2–14

² The wicked are proud and persecute the poor;
  catch them in the traps they have made.
³ The wicked man is proud of his evil desires;
  the greedy man curses and rejects the LORD.

⁶ He says to himself, "I will never fail;
  I will never be in trouble."

⁸ He hides himself in the villages,
  waiting to murder innocent people.
  He spies on his helpless victims;
⁹ he waits in his hiding place like a lion.
  He lies in wait for the poor;
  he catches them in his trap and drags them away.

¹⁰ The helpless victims lie crushed;
  brute strength has defeated them.
¹¹ The wicked man says to himself, "God doesn't care!
  He has closed his eyes and will never see me!"

¹² O Lord, punish those wicked men!
  Remember those who are suffering!
¹³ How can a wicked man despise God
  and say to himself, "He will not punish me"?

¹⁴ But you do see; you take notice of trouble and suffering
  and are always ready to help.

The helpless man commits himself to you;
   you have always helped the needy.

God Hears the Orphan's Cry

PSALM 10:15–18
15 Break the power of wicked and evil men;
      punish them for the wrong they have done
   until they do it no more.

16 The LORD is king forever and ever.
   Those who worship other gods
      will vanish from his land.

17 You will listen, O LORD, to the prayers of the lowly;
      you will hear the cries of the oppressed and the orphans;
      you will judge in their favor,
   so that mortal men may cause terror no more.

No One Like the Lord

PSALM 113:5–9
5 There is no one like the LORD our God.
   He lives in the heights above,
6   but he bends down
      to see the heavens and the earth.
7 He raises the poor from the dust;
   he lifts the needy from their misery
8 and makes them companions of princes,
   the princes of his people.
9 He honors the childless wife in her home;
   he makes her happy by giving her children.

   Praise the LORD!

PROVERBS 15:25
25 The LORD will destroy the homes of arrogant men,
but he will protect a widow's property.

PROVERBS 28:8

⁸ If you get rich by charging interest and taking advantage of people, your wealth will go to someone who is kind to the poor.

ISAIAH 26:5–6

⁵ He has humbled those who were proud;
   he destroyed the strong city they lived in,
   and sent its walls crashing into the dust.
⁶ Those who were oppressed walk over it now
   and trample it under their feet.

When That Day Comes

ISAIAH 29:17–21

¹⁷ As the saying goes, before long the dense forest will become farmland, and the farmland will go back to forest.

¹⁸ When that day comes, the deaf will be able to hear a book being read aloud, and the blind, who have been living in darkness, will open their eyes and see. ¹⁹ Poor and humble people will once again find the happiness which the LORD, the holy God of Israel, gives. ²⁰ It will be the end of those who oppress others and show contempt for God. Every sinner will be destroyed. ²¹ God will destroy those who slander others, those who prevent the punishment of criminals, and those who tell lies to keep honest men from getting justice.

Mary's Song of Praise

LUKE 1:46–55

⁴⁶ Mary said,
   "My heart praises the Lord;
⁴⁷   my soul is glad because of God my Savior,
⁴⁸   for he has remembered me his lowly servant!
   From now on all people will call me happy,

⁴⁹ because of the great things the Mighty God has done for
  me.
His name is holy;
⁵⁰ from one generation to another
  he shows mercy to those who honor him.
⁵¹ He has stretched out his mighty arm
  and scattered the proud with all their plans.
⁵² He has brought down mighty kings from their thrones,
  and lifted up the lowly.
⁵³ He has filled the hungry with good things,
  and sent the rich away with empty hands.
⁵⁴ He has kept the promise he made to our ancestors,
  and has come to the help of his servant Israel.
⁵⁵ He has remembered to show mercy to Abraham
  and to all his descendants forever!"

Happy Are You

LUKE 6:20–25
²⁰ Jesus looked at his disciples and said,
  "Happy are you poor;
    the Kingdom of God is yours!
²¹ "Happy are you who are hungry now;
    you will be filled!
  "Happy are you who weep now;
    you will laugh!
²⁴ "But how terrible for you who are rich now;
    you have had your easy life!
²⁵ "How terrible for you who are full now;
    you will go hungry!
  "How terrible for you who laugh now;
    you will mourn and weep!

WEALTH BY OPPRESSION

The Charge Against Job

JOB 22:5–9

5 No, it's because you have sinned so much;
  it's because of all the evil you do.
6 To make a brother repay you the money he owed,
  you took away his clothes and left him nothing to wear.
7 You refused water to those who were tired,
  and refused to feed those who were hungry.
8 You used your power and your position
  to take over the whole land.
9 You not only refused to help widows,
  but you also robbed and mistreated orphans.

Job's Defense

JOB 23:1–2; 12

1-2 I still rebel and complain against God;
  I cannot keep from groaning.
12 I always do what God commands;
  I follow his will, not my own desires.

JOB 24:1–12

Why doesn't God set a time for judging,
  a day of justice for those who serve him?

2 Men move property lines to get more land;
  they steal sheep and put them with their own flocks.
3 They take donkeys that belong to orphans,
  and keep a widow's ox till she pays her debts.
4 They prevent the poor from getting their rights
  and force the needy to run and hide.

5 So the poor, like wild donkeys,
  search for food in the dry wilderness;
  nowhere else can they find food for their children.

⁶ They have to harvest fields they don't own,
    and gather grapes in wicked men's vineyards.
⁷ At night they sleep with nothing to cover them,
    nothing to keep them from the cold.
⁸ They are drenched by the rain that falls on the mountains,
    and they huddle beside the rocks for shelter.

⁹ Evil men make slaves of fatherless infants
    and take the poor man's children in payment for debts.
¹⁰ But the poor must go out with no clothes to protect them;
    they must go hungry while harvesting wheat.
¹¹ They press olives for oil, and grapes for wine,
    but they themselves are thirsty.
¹² In the cities the wounded and dying cry out,
    but God ignores their prayers.

JOB 24:19–22

¹⁹ As snow vanishes in heat and drought,
    so a sinner vanishes from the land of the living.
²⁰ Not even his mother remembers him now;
    he is eaten by worms and destroyed like a fallen tree.
²¹ That happens because he mistreated widows
    and showed no kindness to childless women.
²² God, in his strength, destroys the mighty;
    God acts—and the wicked man dies.

JOB 29:11–17

¹¹ Everyone who saw me or heard of me
    had good things to say about what I had done.
¹² When the poor cried out, I helped them;
    I gave help to orphans who had nowhere to turn.
¹³ Men who were in deepest misery praised me,
    and I helped widows find security.
¹⁴ I have always acted justly and fairly.
¹⁵ I was eyes for the blind,
    and feet for the lame.
¹⁶ I was like a father to the poor
    and took the side of strangers in trouble.

¹⁷ I destroyed the power of cruel men
and rescued their victims.

Things Go Well for the Wicked

PSALM 37:12–15
¹² The wicked man plots against the good man
and glares at him with hate.
¹³ But the Lord laughs at wicked men,
because he knows they will soon be destroyed.
¹⁴ The wicked draw their swords and bend their bows
to kill the poor and needy,
to slaughter those who do what is right;
¹⁵ but they will be killed by their own swords,
and their bows will be smashed.

PSALM 73:2–20
² But I had nearly lost confidence;
my faith was almost gone
³ because I was jealous of the proud
when I saw that things go well for the wicked.
⁴ They do not suffer pain;
they are strong and healthy.
⁵ They do not suffer as other people do;
they do not have the troubles that others have.
⁶ And so they wear pride like a necklace
and violence like a robe;
⁷ their hearts pour out evil,^z
and their minds are busy with wicked schemes.
⁸ They laugh at other people and speak of evil things;
they are proud and make plans to oppress others.
⁹ They speak evil of God in heaven
and give arrogant orders to men on earth,
¹⁰ so that even God's people turn to them
and eagerly believe whatever they say.^a

¹¹ They say, "God will not know;
the Most High will not find out."

12 That is what the wicked are like.
   They have plenty and are always getting more.
13 Is it for nothing, then, that I have kept myself pure
   and have not committed sin?
14 O God, you have made me suffer all day long;
   every morning you have punished me.
15 If I had said such things,
   I would not be acting as one of your people.
16 I tried to think this problem through,
   but it was too difficult for me
17   until I went into your Temple.
   Then I understood what will happen to the wicked.
18 You will put them in slippery places
   and make them fall to destruction!
19 They are instantly destroyed;
   they go down to a horrible end.
20 They are like a dream that goes away in the morning;
   when you rouse yourself, O Lord, they disappear.

Mocked by Oppressors

PSALM 123:3–4
3 Be merciful to us, LORD, be merciful;
   we have been treated with so much contempt.
4 We have been mocked too long by the rich
   and scorned by proud oppressors.

Riches by Dishonesty

PROVERBS 20:17
   17 What you get by dishonesty you may enjoy like
the finest food, but sooner or later it will be like a mouth-
ful of sand.

PROVERBS 21:6
   6The riches you get by dishonesty soon disappear,
but not before they lead you into the jaws of death.

¹⁶ If you make gifts to rich people or oppress the poor to get rich, you will become poor yourself.

INTRODUCTION TO ISAIAH 3:1,13–25

Due to a temporary pause in the rise of Assyria, Israel and Judah enjoyed a period of security and subsequent prosperity during the first half of the eighth century. But disaster struck in the last third of the century. Israel was destroyed in 721 and Judah was devastated by foreign invasion. The destruction which Amos (2:4–3:2) and Hosea (5:1–15) had foreseen occurred in the time of Isaiah and Micah, whose ministries roughly paralleled each other (from about the middle of the eighth to the beginning of the seventh century).

As Isaiah points out here, the increased wealth enjoyed during the first part of the eighth century was by no means evenly distributed. Rather, the powerful had taken advantage of the weak. Isaiah tells us that the "elders" (representatives of the family clans) and "leaders" (probably government officials) have become rich by oppressing the poor. When Isaiah charges that they "crush"or "grind the faces" of the poor, his language is particularly graphic. The Hebrew verb he employs was often used to describe corn being ground between millstones. Isaiah's condemnation of the arrogant women of "higher society,"infatuated with their sophisticated fashions and costly adornment (vv. 16–24), is similar to that of Amos (4:1–3).

For further study: *in addition to BB, IB, NBC, and NCC, see also G.B. Gray,* A Critical and Exegetical Commentary on the Book of Isaiah, I-XXVII *(ICC, New York: Charles Scribner's Sons, 1912); Otto Kaiser,* Isaiah 1–12 *(Philadelphia: The Westminster Press, 1972).*

ISAIAH 3:1, 13–25

Now the Lord, the Almighty LORD, is about to take away from Jerusalem and Judah everything and everyone that the people depend on. He is going to take away their food and their water.

¹³ The LORD is ready to state his case; he is ready to judge his people.ᵍ ¹⁴ The LORD is bringing the elders and leaders of his people to judgment. He makes this accusation: "You have plundered vineyards, and your houses are full of what you have taken from the poor. ¹⁵ You have no right to crush my people and take advantage of the poor. I, the Sovereign LORD Almighty, have spoken."

¹⁶ The LORD said, "Look how proud the women of Jerusalem are! They walk along with their noses in the air. They are always flirting. They take dainty little steps, and the bracelets on their ankles jingle. ¹⁷ But I will punish them—I will shave their heads and leave them bald."

¹⁸ A day is coming when the Lord will take away from the women of Jerusalem everything they are so proud of—the ornaments they wear on their ankles, on their heads, on their necks, ¹⁹ and on their wrists. He will take away their veils ²⁰ and their hats; the magic charms they wear on their arms and at their waists; ²¹ the rings they wear on their fingers and in their noses; ²² all their fine robes, gowns, cloaks, and purses; ²³ their revealing garments, their linen handkerchiefs, and the scarves and long veils they wear on their heads.

²⁴ Instead of using perfumes, they will stink; instead of fine belts, they will wear coarse ropes; instead of having beautiful hair, they will be bald; instead of fine clothes, they will be dressed in rags; their beauty will be turned to shame!

²⁵ The men of the city, yes, even the strongest men, will be killed in war.

ISAIAH 10:13–19

¹³ The emperor of Assyria boasts, "I have done it all myself. I am strong and wise and clever. I wiped out the boundaries between nations and took the supplies they had stored. Like a bull I have trampled the people who live there. ¹⁴ The nations of the world were like a bird's nest, and I gathered their wealth as easily as gathering eggs. Not a wing fluttered to scare me off; no beak opened to scream at me!"

¹⁵ But the LORD says, "Can an ax claim to be greater than the man who uses it? Is a saw more important than the man who saws with it? A club doesn't lift up a man; a man lifts up a club."

¹⁶ The LORD Almighty is going to send disease to punish those who are now well-fed. In their bodies there will be a fire that burns and burns. ¹⁷ God, the light of Israel, will become a fire. Israel's holy God will become a flame, which in a single day will burn up everything, even the thorns and thistles. ¹⁸ The rich forests and farmlands will be totally destroyed, in the same way that a fatal sickness destroys a man. ¹⁹ There will be so few trees left that even a child will be able to count them.

INTRODUCTION TO JEREMIAH 5:7–9; 26–29

Jeremiah began his prophetic ministry in 626, the thirteenth year of King Josiah. The northern kingdom had fallen to the Assyrians almost a century before. Judah was all that remained of Yahweh's covenant people. That Judah herself would fall also seemed certain. Indeed, during Jeremiah's ministry of over forty years, Judah experienced in one way or another the control of the Assyrians, the Egyptians, and the Babylonians. What troubled Jeremiah, however, was not so much Judah's imminent doom as the religious and moral insensitivity of her people.

This particular prophecy is probably to be dated after Josiah's death in 609—a time when, under the corrupt

King Jehoiakim (see Lesson XII), the moral tone of the nation continually deteriorated. Jeremiah is enraged at the moral callousness and oppression on the part of the wealthy who grow "fat and well-fed" (a description which would have been understood by Jeremiah's audience as an accusation of impiety and self-centeredness). He compares the wicked rich to fowlers, or bird-hunters. They set hidden traps and catch their human prey by deceit. The wealthier Judeans knew the legal structures well and could cleverly exploit the poor within the bounds of the law.

For further study: *in addition to BB, IB, NBC, and NCC, see also John Bright,* Jeremiah *("The Anchor Bible," New York: Doubleday & Co., Inc., 1965); R. K. Harrison,* Jeremiah and Lamentations *(TOT, Downers Grove: Inter-Varsity Press, 1973).*

That Is Why They Are Fat

JEREMIAH 5:7-9; 26-29

7 The LORD asked, "Why should I forgive the sins of my
        people?
    They have abandoned me
        and have worshiped gods that are not real.
    I fed my people until they were full,
        but they committed adultery
        and spent their time with prostitutes.
8 They were like well-fed stallions wild with desire,
        each lusting for his neighbor's wife.
9 Shouldn't I punish them for these things
        and take revenge on a nation such as this?

26 "Evil men live among my people; they lie in wait like men who lay nets to catch birds, but they have set their traps to catch men. 27 Just as a hunter fills his cage with birds, they have filled their houses with loot. That is why they are fat and well fed. There is no limit to their

evil deeds. They do not give orphans their rights or show justice to the oppressed.

²⁹ "But I, the LORD, will punish them for these things; I will take revenge on this nation.

The Wealthy Cheat and Rob

EZEKIEL 22:23–31

²³ The LORD spoke to me again. ²⁴ "Mortal man," he said, "tell the Israelites that their land is unholy, and so I am punishing it in my anger. ²⁵ The leaders^v are like lions roaring over the animals they have killed. They kill the people, take all the money and property they can get, and by their murders leave many widows. ²⁶ The priests break my law and have no respect for what is holy. ²⁷ The government officials are like wolves tearing apart the animals they have killed. They commit murder in order to get rich. ²⁸ The prophets have hidden these sins like men covering a wall with whitewash. They see false visions and make false predictions. They claim to speak the word of the Sovereign LORD, but I, the LORD, have not spoken to them. ²⁹ The wealthy cheat and rob. They mistreat the poor and take advantage of foreigners. ³⁰ I looked for someone who could stand in the places where the walls have crumbled and defend the land when my anger is about to destroy it, but I could find no one. ³¹ So I will turn my anger loose on them, and like a fire I will destroy them for what they have done." The Sovereign LORD has spoken.

HOSEA 12:7–9

⁷ The LORD says, "The people of Israel are as dishonest as the Canaanites; they love to cheat their customers with false scales. ⁸ 'We are rich,' they say. 'We've made a fortune. And no one can accuse us of getting rich dishonestly.' ⁹ But I, the LORD your God who led you out of Egypt, I will make you live in tents again, as you did when I came to you in the desert.

Trampling the Poor

AMOS 8:4–8

⁴ Listen to this, you that trample on the needy and try to destroy the poor of the country. ⁵ You say to yourselves, "We can hardly wait for the holy days to be over so that we can sell our grain. When will the Sabbath end, so that we can start selling again? Then we can overcharge, use false measures, and fix the scales to cheat our customers. ⁶ We can sell worthless wheat at a high price. We'll find a poor man who can't pay his debts, not even the price of a pair of sandals, and we'll buy him as a slave."

⁷ The LORD, the God of Israel, has sworn, "I will never forget their evil deeds. ⁸ And so the earth will quake, and everyone in the land will be in distress. The whole country will be shaken; it will rise and fall like the Nile River.

Your Rich Men Exploit the Poor

MICAH 6:9–15

⁹ It is wise to fear the LORD. He calls to the city, "Listen, you people who assemble in the city! ¹⁰ In the houses of evil men are treasures which they got dishonestly. They use false measures, a thing that I hate. ¹¹ How can I forgive men who use false scales and weights? ¹² Your rich men exploit the poor, and all of you are liars. ¹³ So I have already begunᵏ your ruin and destruction because of your sins. ¹⁴ You will eat, but not be satisfied—in fact you will still be hungry. You will carry things off, but you will not be able to save them; anything you do save I will destroy in war. ¹⁵ You will sow grain, but not harvest the crop. You will press oil from olives, but never get to use it. You will make wine, but never drink it.ˡ

Wealth by Violence

HABAKKUK 2:5–12

⁵ Wealth is deceitful. Greedy men are proud and restless—like death itself they are never satisfied. That is why they [the Babylonians] conquer nation after nation for themselves. ⁶ The conquered people will taunt their conquerors and show their scorn for them. They will say, "You take what isn't yours, but you are doomed! How long will you go on getting rich by forcing your debtors to pay up?"

⁷ But before you know it, you that have conquered others will be in debt yourselves and be forced to pay interest. Enemies will come and make you tremble. They will plunder you! ⁸ You have plundered the people of many nations, but now those who have survived will plunder you because of the murders you have committed and because of your violence against the people of the world and its cities.ᶜ

⁹ You are doomed! You have made your family rich with what you took by violence, and have tried to make your own home safe from harm and danger! ¹⁰ But your schemes have brought shame on your family; by destroying many nations you have only brought ruin on yourself. ¹¹ Even the stones of the walls cry out against you, and the rafters echo the cry.

¹² You are doomed!

Failure To Pay Wages

JAMES 5:1–6

And now, you rich people, listen to me! Weep and wail over the miseries that are coming upon you! ² Your riches have rotted away, and your clothes have been eaten by moths. ³ Your gold and silver are covered with rust, and this rust will be a witness against you and will eat up your flesh like fire. You have piled up riches in these last days. ⁴ You have not paid any wages to the men who work in your fields. Listen to their complaints! The cries of those who gather in your crops have reached the ears of God, the Lord Almighty. ⁵ Your life here on earth has been full of luxury and pleasure. You have made yourselves fat for the day of slaughter. ⁶ You have condemned and murdered innocent people, and they do not resist you.ᶜ

FAILURE TO SHARE

Jerusalem Admonished

EZEKIEL 16:35–50

³⁵ Now then, Jerusalem, you whore! Hear what the LORD is saying.

³⁶ This is what the Sovereign LORD says: "You stripped off your clothes, and like a prostitute, you gave yourself to your lovers and to all your disgusting idols, and you killed your children as sacrifices to idols. ³⁷ Because of this I will bring all your former lovers together—the ones you liked and the ones you hated. I will bring them around you in a circle, and then I will strip off your clothes and let them see you naked. ³⁸ I will condemn you for adultery and murder, and in my anger and fury I will punish you with death. ³⁹ I will put you in their power, and they will tear down the places where you engage in prostitution and worship idols. They will take away your clothes and jewels and leave you completely naked.

⁴⁰ "They will stir up a crowd to stone you, and they will cut you to pieces with their swords. ⁴¹ They will burn your houses down and let crowds of women see your punishment. I will make you stop being a prostitute and make you stop giving gifts to your lovers. ⁴² Then my anger will be over, and I will be calm. I will not be angry or jealous any more. ⁴³ You have forgotten how I treated you when you were young, and you have made me angry

by all the things you did. That is why I have made you pay for them all. Why did you add sexual immorality to all the other disgusting things you did?" The Sovereign LORD has spoken.

The Sin of Sodom

⁴⁴ The LORD said, "People will use this proverb about you, Jerusalem: 'Like mother, like daughter.' ⁴⁵ You really are your mother's daughter. She detested her husband and her children. You are like your sisters, who hated their husbands and their children. You and your sister cities had a Hittite mother and an Amorite[d] father.

⁴⁶ "Your older sister, with her villages, is Samaria, in the north. Your younger sister, with her villages, is Sodom, in the south. ⁴⁷ Were you satisfied to follow in their footsteps and copy their disgusting actions? No, in only a little while you were acting worse than they were in everything you did.

Average Annual Per Capita Cereal Consumption (pounds) (Direct and Indirect), 1964–66 and 1972–74⁹		
	1964–66 average	1972–74 average
United States	1,600	1,850
USSR	1,105	1,435
European Community	900	1,000
Japan	530	620
China	420	430
Developing countries (excluding China)	370	395
Source: Organization for Economic Cooperation and Development		

⁴⁸ "As surely as I am the living God." the Sovereign LORD says, "your sister Sodom and her villages never did the evil that you and your villages have done. ⁴⁹ She and her daughters were proud because they had plenty to eat and lived in peace and quiet, but they did not take care of the poor and the underprivileged. ⁵⁰ They were proud and stubborn and did the things that I hate, so I destroyed them, as you well know.

The Rich Man and Lazarus

LUKE 16:19–31

¹⁹ "There was once a rich man who dressed in the most expensive clothes and lived in great luxury every day. ²⁰ There was also a poor man named Lazarus, covered with sores, who used to be brought to the rich man's door, ²¹ hoping to eat the bits of food that fell from the rich man's table. Even the dogs would come and lick his sores. ²² The poor man died and was carried by the angels to sit beside Abraham at the feast in heaven. The rich man died and was buried, ²³ and in Hades,ˢ where he was in great pain, he looked up and saw Abraham, far away, with Lazarus at his side. ²⁴ So he called out, 'Father Abraham! Take pity on me, and send Lazarus to dip his finger in some water and cool off my tongue, because I am in great pain in this fire!' ²⁵ But Abraham said, 'Remember, my son, that in your lifetime you were given all the good things, while Lazarus got all the bad things. But now he is enjoying himself here, while you are in pain. ²⁶ Besides all that, there is a deep pit lying between us, so that those who want to cross over from here to you cannot do so, nor can anyone cross over to us from where you are.' ²⁷ The rich man said, 'Then I beg you, father Abraham, send Lazarus to my father's house, ²⁸ where I have five brothers. Let him go and warn them so that they, at least, will not come to this place of pain.' ²⁹ Abraham said, 'Your brothers have Moses and the prophets to

warn them; your brothers should listen to what they say.'
³⁰ The rich man answered, 'That is not enough, father
Abraham! But if someone were to rise from death and go
to them, then they would turn from their sins.' ³¹ But
Abraham said, 'If they will not listen to Moses and the
prophets, they will not be convinced even if someone
were to rise from death.' "

GOD'S PEOPLE AND THE POOR

Do Not Mistreat the Weak

PROVERBS 14:21
²¹ If you want to be happy, be kind to the poor; it is a
sin to despise anyone.

EXODUS 22:21–24
²¹ "Do not mistreat or oppress a foreigner; remember
that you were foreigners in Egypt. ²² Do not mistreat any
widow or orphan. ²³ If you do, I, the LORD, will answer
them when they cry out to me for help, ²⁴ and I will become angry and kill you in war. Your wives will become
widows, and your children will be fatherless.

EXODUS 23:9
⁹ "Do not mistreat a foreigner; you know how it feels
to be a foreigner, because you were foreigners in Egypt.

EXODUS 23:12
¹² "Work six days a week, but do no work on the seventh day, so that your slaves and the foreigners who work
for you and even your animals can rest.

LEVITICUS 19:32–34

³² "Show respect for old people and honor them. Reverently obey me; I am the LORD.

³³ "Do not mistreat foreigners who are living in your land. ³⁴ Treat them as you would a fellow Israelite, and love them as you love yourselves. Remember that you were once foreigners in the land of Egypt. I am the LORD your God.

DEUTERONOMY 27:19

¹⁹ " 'God's curse on anyone who deprives foreigners, orphans, and widows of their rights.'

PSALM 41:1–2

Happy are those who are concerned for the poor;
 the LORD will help them when they are in trouble.
² The LORD will protect them and preserve their lives;
 he will make them happy in the land;
 he will not abandon them to the power of their enemies.

God's Will for the King

PSALM 72:1–4

Teach the king to judge with your righteousness, O God;
 share with him your own justice,
² so that he will rule over your people with justice
 and govern the oppressed with righteousness.
³ May the land enjoy prosperity;
 may it experience righteousness.
⁴ May the king judge the poor fairly;
 may he help the needy
 and defeat their oppressors.

PSALM 72:12–14

¹² He rescues the poor who call to him,
 and those who are needy and neglected.
¹³ He has pity on the weak and poor;
 he saves the lives of those in need.

63

¹⁴ He rescues them from oppression and violence;
   their lives are precious to him.

God's Decision

PSALM 82:1–5

God presides in the heavenly council;
   in the assembly of the gods he gives his decision:
² "You must stop judging unjustly;
   you must no longer be partial to the wicked!
³ Defend the rights of the poor and the orphans;
   be fair to the needy and the helpless.
⁴ Rescue them from the power of evil men.
⁵ "How ignorant you are! How stupid!
   You are completely corrupt,
   and justice has disappeared from the world.

An Act of Worship

PROVERBS 14:31

³¹ If you oppress poor people, you insult the God who made them; but kindness shown to the poor is an act of worship.

PROVERBS 21:13

¹³ If you refuse to listen to the cry of the poor, your own cry for help will not be heard.

PROVERBS 22:9

⁹ Be generous and share your food with the poor. You will be blessed for it.

Guard the Rights of the Poor

PROVERBS 22:22–23

²² Don't take advantage of the poor just because you can; don't take advantage of those who stand helpless in

court. ²³ The LORD will argue their case for them and threaten the life of anyone who threatens theirs.

PROVERBS 23:10–11

¹⁰ Never move an old property line or take over land owned by orphans. ¹¹ The LORD is their powerful defender, and he will argue their case against you.

PROVERBS 29:7

⁷ A good person knows the rights of the poor, but wicked people cannot understand such things.

PROVERBS 31:8–9

⁸ "Speak up for people who cannot speak for themselves. Protect the rights of all who are helpless. ⁹ Speak for them and be a righteous judge. Protect the rights of the poor and needy."

Injustice in the World

ECCLESIASTES 4:1

Then I looked again at all the injustice that goes on in this world. The oppressed were crying, and no one would help them. No one would help them, because their oppressors had power on their side.

Do What Is Right

ISAIAH 32:6–8

⁶ A fool speaks foolishly and thinks up evil things to do. What he does and what he says are an insult to the LORD, and he never feeds the hungry or gives thirsty people anything to drink. ⁷ A stupid person is evil and does evil things; he plots to ruin the poor with lies and to keep them from getting their rights. ⁸ But an honorable person acts honestly and stands firm for what is right.

ISAIAH 33:14–16

14 The sinful people of Zion are trembling with fright. They say, "God's judgment is like a fire that burns forever. Can any of us survive a fire like that?" 15 You can survive if you say and do what is right. Don't use your power to cheat the poor and don't accept bribes. Don't join with those who plan to commit murder or to do other evil things. 16 Then you will be safe; you will be as secure as if in a strong fortress. You will have food to eat and water to drink.

JEREMIAH 21:11–12

11-12 The LORD told me to give this message to the royal house of Judah, the descendants of David: "Listen to what I, the LORD, am saying. See that justice is done every day. Protect the person who is being cheated from the one who is cheating him. If you don't, the evil you are doing will make my anger burn like a fire that cannot be put out.

Give to the Poor

LUKE 11:37–41

37 When Jesus finished speaking, a Pharisee invited him to eat with him; so he went in and sat down to eat. 38 The Pharisee was surprised when he noticed that Jesus had not washed before eating. 39 So the Lord said to him, "Now then, you Pharisees clean the outside of your cup and plate, but inside you are full of violence and evil. 40 Fools! Did not God, who made the outside, also make the inside? 41 But give what is in your cups and plates to the poor, and everything will be ritually clean for you.

LUKE 12:32–34

32 "Do not be afraid, little flock, for your Father is pleased to give you the Kingdom. 33 Sell all your belongings and give the money to the poor. Provide for yourselves purses that don't wear out, and save your riches in

heaven, where they will never decrease, because no thief can get to them, and no moth can destroy them. [34] For your heart will always be where your riches are.

LUKE 14:12–14

[12] Then Jesus said to his host, "When you give a lunch or a dinner, do not invite your friends or your brothers or your relatives or your rich neighbors—for they will invite you back, and in this way you will be paid for what you did. [13] When you give a feast, invite the poor, the crippled, the lame, and the blind; [14] and you will be blessed, because they are not able to pay you back. God will repay you on the day the good people rise from the death."

Zacchaeus Repents

LUKE 19:1–10

Jesus went on into Jericho and was passing through. [2] There was a chief tax collector there named Zacchaeus, who was rich. [3] He was trying to see who Jesus was, but he was a little man and could not see Jesus because of the crowd. [4] So he ran ahead of the crowd and climbed a sycamore tree to see Jesus, who was going to pass that way. [5] When Jesus came to that place, he looked up and said to Zacchaeus, "Hurry down, Zacchaeus, because I must stay in your house today."

[6] Zacchaeus hurried down and welcomed him with great joy. [7] All the people who saw it started grumbling, "This man has gone as a guest to the home of a sinner!"

[8] Zacchaeus stood up and said to the Lord, "Listen, sir! I will give half my belongings to the poor, and if I have cheated anyone, I will pay him back four times as much."

[9] Jesus said to him, "Salvation has come to this house today, for this man, also, is a descendant of Abraham. [10] The Son of Man came to seek and to save the lost."

Helping the Poor

³⁶ In Joppa there was a woman named Tabitha, who was a believer. (Her name in Greek is Dorcas, meaning "a deer.") She spent all her time doing good and helping the poor. ³⁷ At that time she got sick and died. Her body was washed and laid in a room upstairs. ³⁸ Joppa was not very far from Lydda, and when the believers in Joppa heard that Peter was in Lydda, they sent two men to him with the message, "Please hurry and come to us." ³⁹ So Peter got ready and went with them. When he arrived, he was taken to the room upstairs, where all the widows crowded around him, crying and showing him all the shirts and coats that Dorcas had made while she was alive. ⁴⁰ Peter put them all out of the room, and knelt down and prayed; then he turned to the body and said, "Tabitha, get up!" She opened her eyes, and when she saw Peter, she sat up. ⁴¹ Peter reached over and helped her get up. Then he called all the believers, including the widows, and presented her alive to them.

Pure Religion

EPHESIANS **4:28**

²⁸ The man who used to rob must stop robbing and start working, in order to earn an honest living for himself and to be able to help the poor.

²⁷ What God the Father considers to be pure and genuine religion is this: to take care of orphans and widows in their suffering and to keep oneself from being corrupted by the world.

A BIBLICAL WARNING TO GOD'S PEOPLE

Worship and Justice

ISAIAH 1:10–17

[10] Jerusalem, your rulers and your people are like those of Sodom and Gomorrah. Listen to what the LORD is saying to you. Pay attention to what our God is teaching you. [11] He says, "Do you think I want all these sacrifices you keep offering to me? I have had more than enough of the sheep you burn as sacrifices and of the fat of your fine animals. I am tired of the blood of bulls and sheep and goats. [12] Who asked you to bring me all this when you come to worship me? Who asked you to do all this tramping around in my Temple? [13] It's useless to bring your offerings. I am disgusted with the smell of the incense you burn. I cannot stand your New Moon Festivals, your Sabbaths, and your religious gatherings; they are all corrupted by your sins. [14] I hate your New Moon Festivals and holy days; they are a burden that I am tired of bearing.

[15] "When you lift your hands in prayer, I will not look at you. No matter how much you pray, I will not listen, for your hands are covered with blood. [16] Wash yourselves clean. Stop all this evil that I see you doing. Yes, stop doing evil [17] and learn to do right. See that justice is done—help those who are oppressed, give orphans their rights, and defend widows."

INTRODUCTION TO ISAIAH 58:1–10

In 538, King Cyrus of Persia, the powerful conqueror of Babylon, declared that the Jews were free to return to Jerusalem to rebuild their temple and disrupted culture. All was not well upon their return, however. For one thing, the exile had left Judah in a state of general confusion and economic instability. Those who had never gone into captivity sometimes viewed the returning exiles as intruders.

Isaiah 58:1–10 seems to speak to this situation of uncertainty and disunity. The prophet's message is clear. While situations may change, Yahweh does not. Religious observance in the context of oppression and neglect of the poor is just as abhorrent to him now as it was before the exile. Therefore God commands the prophet to "shout loudly" in order to shake the people from their misconceived religious practices. Their fasting is unsatisfactory and hypocritical. Apparently they tried to fast and still carry on their unjust business ventures, oppressing their workers (v. 3b). Their fast is unsatisfactory because it misses altogether the connection between devotion to God and concern for the poor. The ritual of fasting calls for self-denial and humiliation before Yahweh. And this must include "removing chains of oppression," sharing "food with the hungry" and offering "homes to the homeless." Jesus says strikingly similar things in Matthew 25:31–46.

For further study: *in addition to BB, IB, NBC, and NCC, see also Christopher R. North, The Second Isaiah (Oxford: The Clarendon Press, 1964); Claus Westermann, Isaiah 40–66, trans. David M.G. Stalker (Philadelphia: The Westminster Press, 1969).*

Fasting and Oppression

ISAIAH 58:1–10

The LORD says, "Shout as loud as you can! Tell my people Israel about their sins! [2] They worship me every day, claiming that they are eager to know my ways and obey my laws. They say they want me to give them just laws and that they take pleasure in worshiping me."

[3] The people ask, "Why should we fast if the LORD never notices? Why should we go without food if he pays no attention?"

The LORD says to them, "The truth is that at the same time you fast, you pursue your own interests and oppress your workers.[4] Your fasting makes you violent, and you quarrel and fight. Do you think this kind of fasting will make me listen to your prayers? [5] When you fast, you make yourselves suffer; you bow your heads low like a blade of grass and spread out sackcloth and ashes to lie on. Is that what you call fasting? Do you think I will be pleased with that?

[6] "The kind of fasting I want is this: Remove the chains of oppression and the yoke of injustice, and let the oppressed go free. [7] Share your food with the hungry and open your homes to the homeless poor. Give clothes to those who have nothing to wear, and do not refuse to help your own relatives.

[8] "Then my favor will shine on you like the morning sun, and your wounds will be quickly healed. I will always be with you to save you; my presence will protect you on every side. [9] When you pray, I will answer you. When you call to me, I will respond.

"If you put an end to oppression, to every gesture of contempt, and to every evil word; [10] if you give food to the hungry and satisfy those who are in need, then the darkness around you will turn to the brightness of noon.

INTRODUCTION TO MATTHEW 25:31–46

This passage depicts the final judgment. All nations will be gathered together, and the righteous will be separated from the cursed in the same way that Palestinian shepherds separated sheep and goats at night (in Jesus' day, sheep and goats were often kept together in the same flock during the day, but were separated at night).

Some have argued that when the text refers to "the least important ones" (v. 45) or "the least important of these brothers of mine" (v. 40), it refers only to believers. But even if the primary reference of these words is to poor believers, other aspects of Jesus' teaching not only permit but also require us to extend the meaning of Matthew 25 to both believers and unbelievers who are poor and oppressed. In the parable of the Good Samaritan (Lk

71

10:29ff) and in Matthew 5:43ff., Jesus corrects the standard of selective love. Instead of loving only our friends, we are to love even our enemies, even those who persecute us. Scripture calls believers to identify not only with oppressed Christians, but also with all poor and oppressed folk.

For further study: *in addition to BB, IB, ICC, NBC, and NCC, see also Eduard Schweitzer,* The Good News According to Matthew, *trans. David E. Green (Atlanta: The John Knox Press, 1957); R. V. G. Tasker,* The Gospel According to St. Matthew *(TNT, Grand Rapids: Eerdmans Pub. Co., 1961).*

The Final Judgment

MATTHEW 25:31–46

[31] "When the Son of Man comes as King and all the angels with him, he will sit on his royal throne, [32] and the people of all the nations will be gathered before him. Then he will divide them into two groups, just as a shepherd separates the sheep from the goats. [33] He will put the righteous people at his right and the others at his left. [34] Then the King will say to the people on his right, 'Come, you that are blessed by my Father! Come and possess the kingdom which has been prepared for you ever since the creation of the world. [35] I was hungry and you fed me, thirsty and you gave me a drink; I was a stranger and you received me in your homes, [36] naked and you clothed me; I was sick and you took care of me, in prison and you visited me.' [37] The righteous will then answer him, 'When, Lord, did we ever see you hungry and feed you, or thirsty and give you a drink? [38] When did we ever see you a stranger and welcome you in our homes, or naked and clothe you? [39] When did we ever see you sick or in prison, and visit you?' [40] The King will reply, 'I tell you, whenever you did this for one of the least important of these brothers of mine, you did it for me!'

[41] "Then he will say to those on his left, 'Away from me, you that are under God's curse! Away to the eternal

fire which has been prepared for the Devil and his angels! 42 I was hungry but you would not feed me, thirsty but you would give me a drink; 43 I was a stranger but you would not welcome me in your homes, naked but you would not clothe me; I was sick and in prison but you would not take care of me.' 44 Then they will answer him, 'When, Lord, did we ever see you hungry or thirsty or a stranger or naked or sick or in prison, and we would not help you?' 45 The King will reply, 'I tell you, whenever you refused to help one of these least important ones, you refused to help me.' 46 These, then, will be sent off to eternal punishment, but the righteous will go to eternal life."

Things That Demonstrate Repentance

LUKE 3:7–11

7 Crowds of people came out to John to be baptized by him. "You snakes!" he said to them. "Who told you that you could escape from the punishment God is about to send? 8 Do those things that will show that you have turned from your sins. And don't start saying among yourselves that Abraham is your ancestor. I tell you that God can take these rocks and make descendants for Abraham! 9 The ax is ready to cut down the trees at the roots; every tree that does not bear good fruit will be cut down and thrown in the fire."

10 The people asked him, "What are we to do, then?"

11 He answered, "Whoever has two shirts must give one to the man who has none, and whoever has food must share it."

Punishment of Religious Leaders

LUKE 20:45–47

45 As all the people listened to him, Jesus said to his disciples, 46 "Be on your guard against the teachers of the Law, who like to walk around in their long robes and

73

love to be greeted with respect in the marketplace; who choose the reserved seats in the synagogues and the best places at feasts; [47] who take advantage of widows and rob them of their homes, and then make a show of saying long prayers! Their punishment will be all the worse!"

Whoever Does Not Love

JAMES 2:14–17

[14] My brothers, what good is it for someone to say that he has faith if his actions do not prove it? Can that faith save him? [15] Suppose there are brothers or sisters who need clothes and don't have enough to eat. [16] What good is there in your saying to them, "God bless you! Keep warm and eat well!"—if you don't give them the necessities of life? [17] So it is with faith: if it is alone and includes no action, then it is dead.

1 JOHN 3:16–18

[16] This is how we know what love is: Christ gave his life for us. We too, then, ought to give our lives for our brothers! [17] If a rich person sees his brother in need, yet closes his heart against his brother, how can he claim that he loves God? [18] My children, our love should not be just words and talk; it must be true love, which shows itself in action.

1 JOHN 4:7–8

[7] Dear friends, let us love one another, because love comes from God. Whoever loves is a child of God and knows God. [8] Whoever does not love does not know God, for God is love.

Children of the Father

MATTHEW 5:43–48

[43] "You have heard that it was said, 'Love your friends, hate your enemies.' [44] But now I tell you: love

your enemies and pray for those who persecute you, [45] so that you may become the sons of your Father in heaven. For he makes his sun to shine on bad and good people alike, and gives rain to those who do good and to those who do evil. [46] Why should God reward you if you love only the people who love you? Even the tax collectors do that! [47] And if you speak only to your friends, have you done anything out of the ordinary? Even the pagans do that! [48] You must be perfect—just as your Father in heaven is perfect.

IS GOD FAIR?

DEUTERONOMY 10:17–19

[17] The LORD your God is supreme over all gods and over all powers. He is great and mighty, and he is to be obeyed. He does not show partiality, and he does not accept bribes. [18] He makes sure that orphans and widows are treated fairly; he loves the foreigners who live with our people, and gives them food and clothes. [19] So then, show love for those foreigners, because you were once foreigners in Egypt.

Justice and Fairness

EXODUS 23:1–3

"Do not spread false rumors, and do not help a guilty man by giving false testimony. [2] Do not follow the majority when they do wrong or when they give testimony that perverts justice. [3] Do not show partiality to a poor man at his trial.

JOB 34:18–19

[18] God condemns kings and rulers
    when they are worthless or wicked.

¹⁹ He does not take the side of rulers
nor favor the rich over the poor,
for he created everyone.

ROMANS 1:14–15

¹⁴ For I have an obligation to all peoples, to the civilized and to the savage, to the educated and to the ignorant. ¹⁵ So then, I am eager to preach the Good News to you also who live in Rome.

III

ECONOMIC RELATIONSHIPS AMONG THE PEOPLE OF GOD: SOME BIBLICAL EXAMPLES

THE YEAR OF RESTORATION (JUBILEE)

NUMBERS 26:52–56

⁵² The Lord said to Moses, ⁵³ "Divide the land among the tribes, according to their size. ⁵⁴⁻⁵⁶ Divide the land by drawing lots, and give a large share to a large tribe and a small one to a small tribe."

INTRODUCTION TO LEV. 25:8ff.

The economic provisions of the Year of Jubilee have sweeping implications. Every forty-nine years, the text declares, slaves are to be set free, debts are to be either suspended or canceled, and land is to be returned to the original owners (although actually this declaration underlines the knowledge that all land ultimately belongs only to Yahweh).

Scholars differ over the conditions under which the Jubilee tradition developed. There is not much evidence that it was implemented. The only other direct scriptural reference to it is found in Numbers 36:4. The term "Jubilee" is derived from the Hebrew word "yobel" (ram's horn). That horn was blown to announce the Year of Jubilee. Since this word was no longer commonly used to designate "trumpet" in later Hebrew, it is quite likely that the tradition had rather early origins. Whatever the date of origin and the degree of implementation, this text remains as a striking part of the Christian canon.

For further study: *In addition to BB, IB, NBC and NCC, see also Roland de Vaux,* Ancient Israel: Its Life and Institutions, *trans. John McHugh (London: Darton, Longman & Todd, 1961); Martin Noth,* Leviticus, *trans. J. E. Anderson (OTL, London: SCM Press, 1965); Robert B. Sloan Jr.,* The Favorable Year of the Lord: A Study of Jubilary Theology in the Gospel of Luke *(Ph.D. disserta-*

tion, University of Basel; Austin, Texas: Schola Press, 1977).

The Year of Restoration

LEVITICUS 25:8–17

⁸ Count seven times seven years, a total of forty-nine years. ⁹ Then, on the tenth day of the seventh month, the Day of Atonement, send a man to blow a trumpet throughout the whole land. ¹⁰ In this way you shall set the fiftieth year apart and proclaim freedom to all the inhabitants of the land. During this year all property that has been sold shall be restored to the original owner or his descendants, and anyone who has been sold as a slave shall return to his family. ¹¹ You shall not plant your fields or harvest the grain that grows by itself or gather the grapes in your unpruned vineyards. ¹² The whole year shall be sacred for you; you shall eat only what the fields produce of themselves.

¹³ In this year all property that has been sold shall be restored to its original owner. ¹⁴ So when you sell land to your fellow Israelite or buy land from him, do not deal unfairly. ¹⁵ The price is to be set according to the number of years the land can produce crops before the next Year of Restoration. ¹⁶ If there are many years, the price shall be higher, but if there are only a few years, the price shall be lower, because what is being sold is the number of crops the land can produce. ¹⁷ Do not cheat a fellow Israelite, but have obedient reverence for the Lord your God.

The Problem of the Seventh Year

LEVITICUS 25:18–34

¹⁸ Obey all the LORD's laws and commands, so that you may live in safety in the land. ¹⁹ The land will produce its crops, and you will have all you want to eat and will live in safety.

²⁰ But someone may ask what there will be to eat during the seventh year, when no fields are planted and no crops gathered. ²¹ The LORD will bless the land in the sixth year so that it will produce enough food for two years. ²² When you plant your fields in the eighth year, you will still be eating what you harvested during the sixth year, and you will have enough to eat until the crops you plant that year are harvested.

Restoration of Property

²³ Your land must not be sold on a permanent basis, because you do not own it; it belongs to God, and you are like foreigners who are allowed to make use of it.

²⁴ When land is sold, the right of the original owner to buy it back must be recognized. ²⁵ If an Israelite becomes poor and is forced to sell his land, his closest relative is to buy it back. ²⁶ A man who has no relative to buy it back may later become prosperous and have enough to buy it back himself. ²⁷ In that case he must pay to the man who bought it a sum that will make up for the years remaining until the next Year of Restoration, when he would in any event recover his land. ²⁸ But if he does not have enough money to buy the land back, it remains under the control of the man who bought it until the next Year of Restoration. In that year it will be returned to its original owner.

²⁹ If a man sells a house in a walled city, he has the right to buy it back during the first full year from the date of sale. ³⁰ But if he does not buy it back within the year, he loses the right of repurchase, and the house becomes the permanent property of the purchaser and his descendants; it will not be returned in the Year of Restoration. ³¹ But houses in unwalled villages are to be treated like fields; the original owner has the right to buy them back, and they are to be returned in the Year of Restoration. ³² However, Levites have the right to buy back at

any time their property in the cities assigned to them. ³³ If a house in one of these cities is sold by a Levite and is not bought back, it must be returned in the Year of Restoration, because the houses which the Levites own in their cities are their permanent property among the people of Israel. ³⁴ But the pasture land around the Levite cities shall never be sold; it is their property forever.

Loans to the Poor

LEVITICUS 25:35–55

³⁵ If a fellow Israelite living near you becomes poor and cannot support himself, you must provide for him as you would for a hired man, so that he can continue to live near you. ³⁶ Do not charge him any interest, but obey God and let your fellow Israelite live near you. ³⁷ Do not make him pay interest on the money you lend him, and do not make a profit on the food you sell him. ³⁸ This is the command of the LORD your God, who brought you out of Egypt in order to give you the land of Canaan and to be your God.

Release of Slaves

³⁹ If a fellow Israelite living near you becomes so poor that he sells himself to you as a slave, you shall not make him do the work of a slave. ⁴⁰ He shall stay with you as a hired man and serve you until the next Year of Restoration. ⁴¹ At that time he and his children shall leave you and return to his family and to the property of his ancestors. ⁴² The people of Israel are the LORD's slaves, and he brought them out of Egypt; they must not be sold into slavery. ⁴³ Do not treat them harshly, but obey your God. ⁴⁴ If you need slaves, you may buy them from the nations around you. ⁴⁵ You may also buy the children of the foreigners who are living among you. Such children born in your land may become your prop-

erty, 46 and you may leave them as an inheritance to your sons, whom they must serve as long as they live. But you must not treat any of your fellow Israelites harshly.

47 Suppose a foreigner living with you becomes rich, while a fellow Israelite becomes poor and sells himself as a slave to that foreigner or to a member of his family. 48 After he is sold, he still has the right to be bought back. One of his brothers 49 or his uncle or his cousin or another of his close relatives may buy him back; or if he himself earns enough, he may buy his own freedom. 50 He must consult the one who bought him, and they must count the years until the next Year of Restoration and must set the price for his release on the basis of the wages paid a hired man. 51-52 He must refund a part of the purchase price according to the number of years left, 53 as if he had been hired on an annual basis. His master must not treat him harshly. 54 If he is not set free in any of these ways, he and his children must be set free in the next Year of Restoration. 55 An Israelite cannot be a permanent slave, because the people of Israel are the LORD's slaves. He brought them out of Egypt; he is the LORD their God.

THE SABBATICAL YEAR

EXODUS 23:10

10 "For six years plant your land and gather in what it produces. 11 But in the seventh year let it rest, and do not harvest anything that grows on it. The poor may eat what grows there, and the wild animals can have what is left. Do the same with your vineyards and your olive trees.

A Complete Rest for the Land

LEVITICUS 25:1–7

The LORD spoke to Moses on Mount Sinai and commanded him ² to give the following regulations to the people of Israel. When you enter the land that the LORD is giving you, you shall honor the LORD by not cultivating the land every seventh year. ³ You shall plant your fields, prune your vineyards, and gather your crops for six years. ⁴ But the seventh year is to be a year of complete rest for the land, a year dedicated to the LORD. Do not plant your fields or prune your vineyards. ⁵ Do not even harvest the grain that grows by itself without being planted, and do not gather the grapes from your unpruned vines; it is a year of complete rest for the land. ⁶ Although the land has not been cultivated during that year, it will provide food for you, your slaves, your hired men, the foreigners living with you, ⁷ your domestic animals, and the wild animals in your fields. Everything that it produces may be eaten.

Cancellation of Debts

DEUTERONOMY 15:1–11

"At the end of every seventh year you are to cancel the debts of those who owe you money. ² This is how it is to be done. Everyone who has lent money to a fellow Israelite is to cancel the debt; he must not try to collect the money; the LORD himself has declared the debt canceled. ³ You may collect what a foreigner owes you, but you must not collect what any of your own people owe you.

⁴ "The LORD your God will bless you in the land that he is giving you. Not one of your people will be poor ⁵ if you obey him and carefully observe everything that I command you today. ⁶ The LORD will bless you, as he has promised. You will lend money to many nations, but you will not have to borrow from any; you will have con-

trol over many nations, but no nation will have control over you.

⁷ "If in any of the towns in the land that the LORD your God is giving you there is a fellow Israelite in need, then do not be selfish and refuse to help him. ⁸ Instead, be generous and lend him as much as he needs. ⁹ Do not refuse to lend him something, just because the year when debts are canceled is near. Do not let such an evil thought enter your mind. If you refuse to make the loan, he will cry out to the LORD against you, and you will be held guilty. ¹⁰ Give to him freely and unselfishly, and the LORD will bless you in everything you do. ¹¹ There will always be some Israelites who are poor and in need, and so I command you to be generous to them.

Release of Slaves

DEUTERONOMY 15:12–15

¹² If a fellow Israelite, man or woman, sells himself to you as a slave, you are to release him after he has served you for six years. When the seventh year comes, you must let him go free. ¹³ When you set him free, do not send him away empty-handed. ¹⁴ Give to him generously from what the LORD has blessed you with—sheep, grain, and wine. ¹⁵ Remember that you were slaves in Egypt and the LORD your God set you free; that is why I am now giving you this command.

A Broken Promise

JEREMIAH 34:8–17

⁸ King Zedekiah and the people of Jerusalem had made an agreement to set free ⁹ their Hebrew slaves, both male and female, so that no one would have a fellow Israelite as a slave. ¹⁰ All the people and their leaders agreed to free their slaves and never to enslave them again. They did set them free, ¹¹ but later they changed their minds, took them back, and forced them to become slaves again.

¹² Then the LORD, ¹³ the God of Israel, told me to say to the people: "I made a covenant with your ancestors when I rescued them from Egypt and set them free from slavery. I told them that ¹⁴ every seven years they were to set free any Hebrew slave who had served them for six years. But your ancestors would not pay any attention to me or listen to what I said.   Just a few days ago you changed your minds and did what pleased me. All of you agreed to set your fellow Israelites free, and you made a covenant in my presence, in the Temple where I am worshiped. ¹⁶ But then you changed your minds again and dishonored me. All of you took back the slaves whom you had set free as they desired, and you forced them into slavery again. ¹⁷ So now, I, the LORD, say that you have disobeyed me; you have not given your fellow Israelites their freedom. Very well, then I will give you freedom: the freedom to die by war, disease, and starvation. I will make every nation in the world horrified at what I do to you.

Failure To Observe the Seventh Year

2 CHRONICLES 36:17–21
¹⁷ So the LORD brought the king of Babylonia to attack them. ¹⁹ He burned down the Temple and the city, with all its palaces and its wealth, and broke down the city wall. ²⁰ He took all the survivors to Babylonia, where they served him and his descendants as slaves until the rise of the Persian Empire. ²¹ And so what the LORD had foretold through the prophet Jeremiah was fulfilled: "The land will lie desolate for seventy years, to make up for the Sabbath rest ⁵ that has not been observed."

A New Commitment

NEHEMIAH 10:28–31
²⁸ We, the people of Israel, the priests, the Levites, the Temple guards, the Temple musicians, the Temple

workmen, and all others who in obedience to God's law have separated themselves from the foreigners living in our land, we, together with our wives and all our children old enough to understand, ²⁹ do hereby join with our leaders in an oath, under penalty of a curse if we break it, that we will live according to God's Law, which God gave through his servant Moses; that we will obey all that the LORD, our God, commands us; and that we will keep all his laws and requirements.

Every seventh year we will not farm the land, and we will cancel all debts.

TITHING

You Will Be My God

GENESIS 28:20-22
²⁰ Then Jacob made a vow to the LORD: "If you will be with me and protect me on the journey I am making and give me food and clothing, ²¹ and if I return safely to my father's home, then you will be my God. ²² This memorial stone which I have set up will be the place where you are worshiped, and I will give you a tenth of everything you give me."

LEVITICUS 27:32
When the animals are counted, every tenth one belongs to the LORD.

DEUTERONOMY 14:22-29
²² "Set aside a tithe—a tenth of all that your fields produce each year. ²³ Then go to the one place where the LORD your God has chosen to be worshiped; and there in his presence eat the tithes of your grain, wine, and olive

oil, and the first-born of your cattle and sheep. Do this so that you may learn to have reverence for the LORD your God always. ²⁴ If the place of worship is too far from your home for you to carry there the tithe of the produce that the LORD has blessed you with, then do this: ²⁵ Sell your produce and take the money with you to the one place of worship. ²⁶ Spend it on whatever you want—beef, lamb, wine, beer—and there, in the presence of the LORD your God, you and your families are to eat and enjoy yourselves.

²⁷ "Do not neglect the Levites who live in your towns; they have no property of their own. ²⁸ At the end of every third year bring the tithe of all your crops and store it in your towns. ²⁹ This food is for the Levites, since they own no property, and for the foreigners, orphans, and widows who live in your towns. They are to come and get all they need. Do this, and the LORD your God will bless you in everything you do.

DEUTERONOMY 26:12–13

¹² "Every third year give the tithe—a tenth of your crops—to the Levites, the foreigners, the orphans, and the widows, so that in every community they will have all they need to eat. When you have done this, ¹³ say to the LORD, 'None of the sacred tithe is left in my house; I have given it to the Levites, the foreigners, the orphans, and the widows, as you commanded me to do. I have not disobeyed or forgotten any of your commands concerning the tithe.

Tithing, Justice and Love

LUKE 11:42

⁴² "How terrible for you Pharisees! You give to God one tenth of the seasoning herbs, such as mint and rue and all the other herbs, but you neglect justice and love for God. These you should practice, without neglecting the others.

LAWS FOR HARVESTERS

Grain for the Poor

LEVITICUS 19:9–10

⁹ "When you harvest your fields, do not cut the grain at the edges of the fields, and do not go back to cut the heads of grain that were left. ¹⁰ Do not go back through your vineyard to gather the grapes that were missed or to pick up the grapes that have fallen; leave them for poor people and foreigners. I am the LORD your God.

LEVITICUS 23:22

²² When you harvest your fields, do not cut the grain at the edges of the fields, and do not go back to cut the heads of grain that were left; leave them for poor people and foreigners. The LORD is your God.

DEUTERONOMY 24:19–22

¹⁹ "When you gather your crops and fail to bring in some of the grain that you have cut, do not go back for it; it is to be left for the foreigners, orphans, and widows, so that the LORD your God will bless you in everything you do. ²⁰ When you have picked your olives once, do not go back and get those that are left; they are for the foreigners, orphans, and widows. ²¹ When you have gathered your grapes once, do not go back over the vines a second time; the grapes that are left are for the foreigners, orphans, and widows. ²² Never forget that you were slaves in Egypt; that is why I have given you this command.

Ruth Works in the Field of Boaz

Naomi had a relative named Boaz, a rich and influential man who belonged to the family of her husband Elimelech. ² One day Ruth said to Naomi, "Let me go to the fields to gather the grain that the harvest workers leave. I am sure to find someone who will let me work with him."

Naomi answered, "Go ahead, daughter."

³ So Ruth went out to the fields and walked behind the workers, picking up the heads of grain which they left. It so happened that she was in a field that belonged to Boaz.

⁴ Some time later Boaz himself arrived from Bethlehem and greeted the workers. "The LORD be with you!" he said.

"The LORD bless you!" they answered.

⁵ Boaz asked the man in charge, "Who is that young woman?"

⁶ The man answered, "She is the foreign girl who came back from Moab with Naomi. ⁷ She asked me to let her follow the workers and gather grain. She has been working since early morning and has just now stopped to rest for a while under the shelter."

⁸ Then Boaz said to Ruth, "Let me give you some advice. Don't gather grain anywhere except in this field. Work with the women here; ⁹ watch them to see where they are reaping and stay with them. I have ordered my men not to molest you. And whenever you are thirsty, go and drink from the water jars that they have filled."

ON CHARGING INTEREST

On Lending Money

EXODUS 22:25–27

²⁵ "If you lend money to any of my people who are poor, do not act like a moneylender and require him to pay interest. ²⁶ If you take someone's cloak as a pledge that he will pay you, you must give it back to him before the sun sets, ²⁷ because it is the only covering he has to keep him warm. What else can he sleep in? When he cries out to me for help, I will answer him because I am merciful.

DEUTERONOMY 23:19–20

¹⁹ "When you lend money or food or anything else to a fellow Israelite, do not charge him interest. ²⁰ You may charge interest on what you lend to a foreigner, but not on what you lend to a fellow Israelite. Obey this rule, and the LORD your God will bless everything you do in the land that you are going to occupy.

Oppression of the Poor

NEHEMIAH 5:1–12

Some time later many of the people, both men and women, began to complain against their fellow Jews. ² Some said, "We have large families, we need grain to keep us alive."

³ Others said, "We have had to mortgage our fields and vineyards and houses to get enough grain to keep us from starving."

⁴ Still others said, "We had to borrow money to pay the royal tax on our fields and vineyards. ⁵ We are of the same race as our fellow Jews. Aren't our children just as

good as theirs? But we have to make slaves of our children. Some of our daughters have already been sold as slaves. We are helpless because our fields and vineyards have been taken away from us."

⁶ When I heard their complaints, I grew angry ⁷ and decided to act. I denounced the leaders and officials of the people and told them, "You are oppressing your brothers!"

I called a public assembly to deal with the problem ⁸ and said, "As far as we have been able, we have been buying back our Jewish brothers who had to sell themselves to foreigners. Now you are forcing your own brothers to sell themselves to you, their fellow Jews!" The leaders were silent and could find nothing to say.

⁹ Then I said, "What you are doing is wrong! You ought to have reverence for God and do what's right. Then you would not give our enemies, the Gentiles, any reason to ridicule us. ¹⁰ I have let the people borrow money and grain from me, and so have my companions and the men who work for me. Now let's give up all our claims to repayment. ¹¹ Cancel all the debts they owe you—money or grain or wine or olive oil. And give them back their fields, vineyards, olive groves, and houses right now!"

¹² The leaders replied, "We'll do as you say. We'll give the property back and not try to collect the debts."

Doing What Is Right

PSALM 15:1–5

LORD, who may enter your Temple?
Who may worship on Zion,
   your sacred hill?
² A person who obeys God in everything
   and always does what is right,
whose words are true and sincere,
³   and who does not slander others.

He always does what he promises,
no matter how much it may cost.
⁵ He makes loans without charging interest
and cannot be bribed to testify against the innocent.

JESUS' NEW COMMUNITY

Salt and Light

MATTHEW 5:13–16

¹³ "You are like salt for all mankind. But if salt loses
its saltiness, there is no way to make it salty again. It has
become worthless, so it is thrown out and people trample
on it.

¹⁴ "You are like light for the whole world. A city
built on a hill cannot be hid. ¹⁵ No one lights a lamp and
puts it under a bowl; instead he puts it on the lampstand,
where it gives light for everyone in the house. ¹⁶ In the
same way your light must shine before people, so that
they will see the good things you do and praise your Father in heaven.

Teaching about Charity

MATTHEW 6:1–4

"Make certain you do not perform your religious
duties in public so that people will see what you do. If
you do these things publicly, you will not have any reward from your Father in heaven.

² "So when you give something to a needy person, do
not make a big show of it, as the hypocrites do in the
houses of worship and on the streets. They do it so that
people will praise them. I assure you, they have already
been paid in full. ³ But when you help a needy person, do
it in such a way that even your closest friend will not

know about it. ⁴ Then it will be a private matter. And your Father, who sees what you do in private, will reward you.

Receiving a Hundred Times More

MARK 10:28–31; 35–45

²⁸ Then Peter spoke up, "Look, we have left everything and followed you."

²⁹ "Yes," Jesus said to them, "and I tell you that anyone who leaves home or brothers or sisters or mother or father or children or fields for me and for the gospel, ³⁰ will receive much more in this present age. He will receive a hundred times more houses, brothers, sisters, mothers, children, and fields—and persecutions as well; and in the age to come he will receive eternal life. ³¹ But many who are now first will be last, and many who are now last will be first."

³⁵ Then James and John, the sons of Zebedee, came to Jesus. "Teacher," they said, "there is something we want you to do for us."

³⁶ "What is it?" Jesus asked them.

³⁷ They answered, "When you sit on your throne in your glorious Kingdom, we want you to let us sit with you, one at your right and one at your left."

³⁸ Jesus said to them, "You don't know what you are asking for. Can you drink the cup of suffering that I must drink? Can you be baptized in the way I must be baptized?"

³⁹ "We can," they answered.

Jesus said to them, "You will indeed drink the cup I must drink and be baptized in the way I must be baptized. ⁴⁰ But I do not have the right to choose who will sit at my right and my left. It is God who will give these places to those for whom he has prepared them."

⁴¹ When the other ten disciples heard about it, they became angry with James and John. ⁴² So Jesus called them all together to him and said, "You know that the

men who are considered rulers of the heathen have power over them, and the leaders have complete authority. [43] This, however, is not the way it is among you. If one of you wants to be great, he must be the servant of the rest; [44] and if one of you wants to be first, he must be the slave of all. [45] For even the Son of Man did not come to be served; he came to serve and to give his life to redeem many people."

Jesus' Helpers

MARK 15:40–41

[40] Some women were there, looking on from a distance. Among them were Mary Magdalene, Mary the mother of the younger James and of Joseph, and Salome. [41] They had followed Jesus while he was in Galilee and had helped him. Many other women who had come to Jerusalem with him were there also.

LUKE 8:1–3

Some time later Jesus traveled through towns and villages, preaching the Good News about the Kingdom of God. The twelve disciples went with him, [2] and so did some women who had been healed of evil spirits and diseases: Mary (who was called Magdalene), from whom seven demons had been driven out; [3] Joanna, whose husband Chuza was an officer in Herod's court; and Susanna, and many other women who used their own resources to help Jesus and his disciples.

The Lord's Supper

LUKE 22:14–20

[14] When the hour came, Jesus took his place at the table with the apostles. [15] He said to them, "I have wanted so much to eat this Passover meal with you before I suffer! [16] For I tell you, I will never eat it until it is given its full meaning in the Kingdom of God."

[17] Then Jesus took a cup, gave thanks to God, and said, "Take this and share it among yourselves. [18] I tell you that from now on I will not drink this wine until the Kingdom of God comes."

[19] Then he took a piece of bread, gave thanks to God, broke it, and gave it to them, saying, "This is my body, which is given for you. Do this in memory of me." [20] In the same way, he gave them the cup after the supper, saying, "This cup is God's new covenant sealed with my blood, which is poured out for you."

Jesus Washes His Disciples' Feet

JOHN 13:1–17

It was now the day before the Passover Festival. Jesus knew that the hour had come for him to leave this world and go to the Father. He had always loved those in the world who were his own, and he loved them to the very end.

[2] Jesus and his disciples were at supper. The Devil had already put the thought of betraying Jesus into the heart of Judas, the son of Simon Iscariot. [3] Jesus knew that the Father had given him complete power; he knew that he had come from God and was going to God. [4] So he rose from the table, took off his outer garment, and tied a towel around his waist. [5] Then he poured some water into a washbasin and began to wash the disciples' feet and dry them with the towel around his waist. [6] He came to Simon Peter, who said to him, "Are you going to wash my feet, Lord?"

[7] Jesus answered him, "You do not understand now what I am doing, but you will understand later."

[8] Peter declared, "Never at any time will you wash my feet!"

"If I do not wash your feet," Jesus answered, "you will no longer be my disciple."

[9] Simon Peter answered, "Lord, do not wash only my feet, then! Wash my hands and head, too!"

¹⁰ Jesus said, "Anyone who has taken a bath is completely clean and does not have to wash himself, except for his feet. All of you are clean—all except one." (¹¹ Jesus already knew who was going to betray him; that is why he said, "All of you, except one, are clean.")

¹² After Jesus had washed their feet, he put his outer garment back on and returned to his place at the table. "Do you understand what I have just done to you?" he asked. ¹³ "You call me Teacher and Lord, and it is right that you do so, because that is what I am. ¹⁴ I, your Lord and Teacher, have just washed your feet. You, then, should wash one another's feet. ¹⁵ I have set an example for you, so that you will do just what I have done for you. ¹⁶ I am telling you the truth: no slave is greater than his master, and no messenger is greater than the one who sent him. ¹⁷ Now that you know this truth, how happy you will be if you put it into practice!

Judas and the Money Bag

JOHN 12:6

⁶ He said this, not because he cared about the poor, but because he was a thief. He carried the money bag and would help himself from it.

JOHN 13:29

²⁹ Since Judas was in charge of the money bag, some of the disciples thought that Jesus had told him to go and buy what they needed for the festival, or to give something to the poor.

Love One Another

JOHN 13:34–35

³⁴ "And now I give you a new commandment: love one another. As I have loved you, so you must love one another. ³⁵ If you have love for one another, then everyone will know that you are my disciples."

THE EARLIEST CHRISTIAN COMMUNITY

Fellowship Among Believers

ACTS 2:41–47

⁴¹ Many of them believed his message and were baptized, and about three thousand people were added to the group that day. ⁴² They spent their time in learning from the apostles, taking part in the fellowship, and sharing in the fellowship meals and the prayers.

⁴³ Many miracles and wonders were being done through the apostles, and everyone was filled with awe. ⁴⁴ All the believers continued together in close fellowship and shared their belongings with one another. ⁴⁵ They would sell their property and possessions, and distribute the money among all, according to what each one needed. ⁴⁶ Day after day they met as a group in the Temple, and they had their meals together in their homes, eating with glad and humble hearts, ⁴⁷ praising God, and enjoying the good will of all the people. And every day the Lord added to their group those who were being saved.

Each According to His Need

INTRODUCTION TO ACTS 4:32–37

Acts 4:32–35 and 2:44–45 describe the economic sharing in the earliest Christian community in Jerusalem. The extensive sharing rose out of a deep unity of fellowship (4:32) and resulted in the satisfaction of everyone's needs (4:34).

Giving was not compulsory (5:1ff). Nor were all possessions turned over to the community. The imperfect verb tense (carried in this translation by the term "would" in 2:45 and 4:34b) suggests repeated acts of sharing whenever

97

there was need rather than one automatic transfer of all possessions to a common purse.

The text seems to connect the economic sharing with the power of the apostolic proclamation of the resurrection of Jesus (4:33). If Jesus proclaimed the Jubilee as part of his proclamation of the Messianic age (see Lesson II), then the dramatic economic sharing occurring in the Jerusalem church would be evidence that they understood his resurrection as a sign that the messianic age had begun.

For further study: *in addition to BB, IB, NBC, and NCC, see also E. M. Blaiklock,* The Acts of the Apostles *(TNT, Grand Rapids: Eerdmans Publishing Company, 1959); F. F. Bruce,* The Acts of the Apostles *(Chicago: Inter-Varsity Christian Fellowship, 1951); Ernst Haenchen,* The Acts of the Apostles, *trans. Bernard Noble, et al. (Philadelphia: The Westminster Press, 1971; Johannes Munck,* The Acts of the Apostles *("The Anchor Bible," Garden City: Doubleday & Co., 1967).*

Each According to His Need

ACTS 4:32–37

³² The group of believers was one in mind and heart. No one said that any of his belongings was his own, but they all shared with one another everything they had. ³³ With great power the apostles gave witness to the resurrection of the Lord Jesus, and God poured rich blessings on them all. ³⁴ There was no one in the group who was in need. Those who owned fields or houses would sell them, bring the money received from the sale, ³⁵ and turn it over to the apostles; and the money was distributed to each one according to his need.

³⁶ And so it was that Joseph, a Levite born in Cyprus, whom the apostles called Barnabas (which means "One who Encourages"), ³⁷ sold a field he owned, brought the money, and turned it over to the apostles.

Neglected Widows

ACTS 6:1–7

Sometime later, as the number of disciples kept growing, there was a quarrel between the Greek-speaking Jews and the native Jews. The Greek-speaking Jews claimed that their widows were being neglected in the daily distribution of funds. [2] So the twelve apostles called the whole group of believers together and said, "It is not right for us to neglect the preaching of God's word in order to handle finances. [3] So then, brothers, choose seven men among you who are known to be full of the Holy Spirit and wisdom, and we will put them in charge of this matter. [4] We ourselves, then, will give our full time to prayer and the work of preaching."

[5] The whole group was pleased with the apostles' proposal, so they chose Stephen, a man full of faith and the Holy Spirit, and Philip, Prochorus, Nicanor, Timon, Parmenas, and Nicolaus, a Gentile from Antioch who had earlier been converted to Judaism. [6] The group presented them to the apostles, who prayed and placed their hands on them.

[7] And so the word of God continued to spread. The number of disciples in Jerusalem grew larger and larger, and a great number of priests accepted the faith.

Aiding Fellow Believers

ACTS 11:27–30

[27] About that time some prophets went from Jerusalem to Antioch. [28] One of them, named Agabus, stood up and by the power of the Spirit predicted that a severe famine was about to come over all the earth. (It came when Claudius was emperor.) [29] The disciples decided that each of them would send as much as he could to help their fellow believers who lived in Judea. [30] They did this, then, and sent the money to the church elders by Barnabas and Saul.

ST. PAUL'S COLLECTION FOR THE POOR
CHRISTIANS AT JERUSALEM

1 CORINTHIANS 16:1–4
Now, concerning what you wrote about the money to be raised to help God's people in Judea. You must do what I told the churches in Galatia to do. ² Every Sunday each of you must put aside some money, in proportion to what he has earned, and save it up, so that there will be no need to collect money when I come. ³ After I come, I shall give letters of introduction to the men you have approved, and send them to take your gift to Jerusalem. ⁴ If it seems worthwhile for me to go, then they can go along with me.

Going to Jerusalem

ACTS 21:10–14
¹⁰ We had been there for several days when a prophet named Agabus arrived from Judea. ¹¹ He came to us, took Paul's belt, tied up his own feet and hands with it, and said, "This is what the Holy Spirit says: The owner of this belt will be tied up in this way by the Jews in Jerusalem, and they will hand him over to the Gentiles."

¹² When we heard this, we and the others there begged Paul not to go to Jerusalem. ¹³ But he answered, "What are you doing, crying like this and breaking my heart? I am ready not only to be tied up in Jerusalem but even to die there for the sake of the Lord Jesus."

¹⁴ We could not convince him, so we gave up and said, "May the Lord's will be done."

ACTS 24:10–14; 17
¹⁰ The governor then motioned to Paul to speak, and Paul said,

"I know that you have been a judge over this nation for many years, and so I am happy to defend myself before you. [11] As you can find out for yourself, it was no more than twelve days ago that I went to Jerusalem to worship. [12] The Jews did not find me arguing with anyone in the Temple, nor did they find me stirring up the people, either in the synagogues or anywhere else in the city. [13] Nor can they give you proof of the accusations they now bring against me. [14] I do admit this to you: I worship the God of our ancestors by following that Way which they say is false. But I also believe in everything written in the Law of Moses and the books of the prophets.

[17] "After being away from Jerusalem for several years, I went there to take some money to my own people and to offer sacrifices.

ROMANS 15:25–29

[25] "Right now, however, I am going to Jerusalem in the service of God's people there. [26] For the churches in Macedonia and Achaia have freely decided to give an offering to help the poor among God's people in Jerusalem. [27] That decision was their own; but as a matter of fact, they have an obligation to help them. Since the Jews shared their spiritual blessings with the Gentiles, the Gentiles ought to use their material blessings to help the Jews. [28] When I have finished this task and have turned over to them all the money that has been raised for them, I shall leave for Spain and visit you on my way there. [29] When I come to you, I know that I shall come with a full measure of the blessing of Christ.

Giving Generously

INTRODUCTION TO 2 CORINTHIANS 8:1–15

Many unusual factors produced poverty in the Jerusalem church. The Roman historians Suetonius and Tacitus, and the Jewish historian Josephus, all report that severe famine struck Palestine in the middle of the first century. Acts 11:27–30 also mentions famine in Judea.

The poverty of the Jerusalem church was also related to peculiar conditions in Jerusalem, especially the city's large number of poor pilgrims. The Jews considered Jerusalem the holy city. Hence large numbers of elderly poor flocked there to die. Also, the Holy City was the favorite location for the rabbis and their students who were dependent on charity. Since almsgiving in Yahweh's city was thought to be an especially meritorious act, the poor in general naturally drifted to Jerusalem. If the Christians there followed Christ's pattern in responding directly and sacrificially to the poor, as we may well suspect they did, it is no wonder that severe financial need surfaced in the Jerusalem church.

Verses 1–2 indicate that the Macedonians had responded to the poverty of their brothers and sisters in Jerusalem with great generosity. These Macedonian churches (i.e., Philippi, Thessalonica, and Beroea) were themselves under serious economic strain. Rome had crippled that area with severe taxes. It is also likely that these Christians, like their brothers and sisters in Jerusalem, experienced considerable persecution (including perhaps discrimination in employment) for their faith. Nevertheless, they responded with joyful, sacrificial generosity to the greater need in Jerusalem.

And so Paul appeals to Corinth as well to respond to Jerusalem's need. In verse 15 he quotes Exodus 16:18, the account of the gathering of manna from heaven. There God commanded that the manna be distributed equally. No one is to have too much and no one is to have too little. In the same spirit, the model for the followers of Christ, as Paul points out to the Corinthians, is indeed the sacrificial Lord himself (v. 9).

For further study: *in addition to BB, IB, NBC, and NCC, see also Murray J. Harris, "II Corinthians," in Frank E. Gaebelein, editor,* The Expositor's Bible Commentary, *Vol. 10 (Grand Rapids: Zondervan Pub. House,*

1976); A. C. Plummer, A Critical and Exegetical Commentary on the Second Epistle of St. Paul to the Corinthians (ICC, Naperville, Ill.: Alec R. Allenson, Inc., 1946); R. V. G. Tasker, The Second Epistle of Paul to the Corinthians (TNT, Grand Rapids: Eerdmans Pub. Co., 1958).

2 CORINTHIANS 8:1–15

Our brothers, we want you to know what God's grace has accomplished in the churches in Macedonia. [2] They have been severely tested by the troubles they went through; but their joy was so great that they were extremely generous in their giving, even though they are very poor. [3] I can assure you that they gave as much as they could, and even more than they could. Of their own free will [4] they begged us and pleaded for the privilege of having a part in helping God's people in Judea. [5] It was more than we could have hoped for! First, they gave themselves to the Lord; and then, by God's will they gave themselves to us as well. [6] So we urged Titus, who began this work, to continue it and help you complete this special service of love. [7] You are so rich in all you have: in faith, speech, and knowledge, in your eagerness to help and in your love for us. And so we want you to be generous also in this service of love.

[8] I am not laying down any rules. But by showing how eager others are to help, I am trying to find out how real your own love is. [9] You know the grace of our Lord Jesus Christ; rich as he was, he made himself poor for your sake, in order to make you rich by means of his poverty.

[10] My opinion is that it is better for you to finish now what you began last year. You were the first, not only to act, but also to be willing to act. [11] On with it, then, and finish the job! Be as eager to finish it as you were to plan it, and do it with what you now have. [12] If you are eager to give, God will accept your gift on the basis of what you have to give, not on what you don't have.

[13-14] I am not trying to relieve others by putting a

Percentage of Disposable Income Spent on Food			
United States	17%	Indonesia	50%
Great Britain	22%	Peru	52%
Japan	23%	Zaire (Congo)	62%
Soviet Union	38%	India	67%

Source: Simon, *Bread for the World*, p. 40.

burden on you; but since you have plenty at this time, it is only fair that you should help those who are in need. Then, when you are in need and they have plenty, they will help you. In this way both are treated equally. [15] As the scripture says, "The one who gathered much did not have too much, and the one who gathered little did not have too little."

Giving Gladly

2 CORINTHIANS 9:1–15

There is really no need for me to write you about the help being sent to God's people in Judea. [2] I know that you are willing to help, and I have boasted of you to the people in Macedonia. "The brothers in Achaia," I said, "have been ready to help since last year." Your eagerness has stirred up most of them. [3] Now I am sending these brothers, so that our boasting about you in this matter may not turn out to be empty words. But, just as I said, you will be ready with your help. [4] However, if the people from Macedonia should come with me and find out that you are not ready, how ashamed we would be—not to speak of your shame—for feeling so sure of you! [5] So I thought it was necessary to urge these brothers to go to you ahead of me and get ready in advance the gift you promised to make. Then it will be ready when I arrive, and it will show that you give because you want to, not because you have to.

⁶ Remember that the person who plants few seeds will have a small crop; the one who plants many seeds will have a large crop. ⁷ Each one should give, then, as he has decided, not with regret or out of a sense of duty; for God loves the one who gives gladly. ⁸ And God is able to give you more than you need, so that you will always have all you need, so that you will always have all you need for yourselves and more than enough for every good cause. ⁹ As the scripture says,

> "He gives generously to the needy;
> his kindness lasts forever."

¹⁰ And God, who supplies seed for the sower and bread to eat, will also supply you with all the seed you need and will make it grow and produce a rich harvest from your generosity. ¹¹ He will always make you rich enough to be generous at all times, so that many will thank God for your gifts which they receive from us. ¹² For this service you perform not only meets the needs of God's people, but also produces an outpouring of grateful thanks to God. ¹³ And because of the proof which this service of yours brings, many will give glory to God for your loyalty to the gospel of Christ, which you profess, and for your generosity in sharing with them and everyone else. ¹⁴ And so with deep affection they will pray for you because of the extraordinary grace God has shown you. ¹⁵ Let us thank God for his priceless gift!

Remembering the Needy

GALATIANS 2:7–10

⁷ On the contrary, they saw that God had given me the task of preaching the gospel to the Gentiles, just as he had given Peter the task of preaching the gospel to the

Jews. [8] For by God's power I was made an apostle to the Gentiles, just as Peter was made an apostle to the Jews. [9] James, Peter, and John, who seemed to be the leaders, recognized that God had given me this special task; so they shook hands with Barnabas and me, as a sign that we were all partners. We agreed that Barnabas and I would work among the Gentiles and they among the Jews. [10] All they asked was that we should remember the needy in their group, which is the very thing I have been eager to do.

FELLOWSHIP IN CHRIST'S BODY

One Body in Christ

ROMANS 12:9–13; 16–17

[9] Love must be completely sincere. Hate what is evil, hold on to what is good. [10] Love one another warmly as Christian brothers, and be eager to show respect for one another. [11] Work hard and do not be lazy. Serve the Lord with a heart full of devotion. [12] Let your hope keep you joyful, be patient in your troubles, and pray at all times. [13] Share your belongings with your needy fellow Christians, and open your homes to strangers.

The cup we use in the Lord's Supper and for which we give thanks to God: when we drink from it, we are sharing in the blood of Christ. And the bread we break: when we eat it, we are sharing in the body of Christ. [17] Because there is the one loaf of bread, all of us, though many, are one body, for we all share the same loaf.

Dishonoring the Lord's Supper

1 CORINTHIANS 11:17–34

¹⁷ In the following instructions, however, I do not praise you, because your meetings for worship actually do more harm than good. ¹⁸ In the first place, I have been told that there are opposing groups in your meetings; and this I believe is partly true. (¹⁹ No doubt there must be divisions among you so that the ones who are in the right may be clearly seen.) ²⁰ When you meet together as a group, it is not the Lord's Supper that you eat. ²¹ For as you eat, each one goes ahead with his own meal, so that some are hungry while others get drunk. ²² Don't you have your own homes in which to eat and drink? Or would you rather despise the church of God and put to shame the people who are in need? What do you expect me to say to you about this? Shall I praise you? Of course I don't!

²³ For I received from the Lord the teaching that I passed on to you: that the Lord Jesus, on the night he was betrayed, took a piece of bread, ²⁴ gave thanks to God, broke it, and said, "This is my body, which is for you. Do this in memory of me." ²⁵ In the same way, after the supper he took the cup and said, "This cup is God's new covenant, sealed with my blood. Whenever you drink it, do so in memory of me."

²⁶ This means that every time you eat this bread and drink from this cup you proclaim the Lord's death until he comes. ²⁷ It follows that if anyone eats the Lord's bread or drinks from his cup in a way that dishonors him, he is guilty of sin against the Lord's body and blood. ²⁸ So then, everyone should examine himself first, and then eat the bread and drink from the cup. ²⁹ For if he does not recognize the meaning of the Lord's body when he eats the bread and drinks from the cup, he brings judgment on himself as he eats and drinks. ³⁰ That is why many of you are sick and weak, and several have died. ³¹ If we would examine ourselves first, we would not

come under God's judgment. [32] But we are judged and punished by the Lord, so that we shall not be condemned together with the world.

[33] So then, my brothers, when you gather together to eat the Lord's Supper, wait for one another. [34] And if anyone is hungry, he should eat at home, so that you will not come under God's judgment as you meet together. As for the other matters, I will settle them when I come.

The Qualities of Love

1 CORINTHIANS 13:1–7

I may be able to speak the languages of men and even of angels, but if I have no love, my speech is no more than a noisy bong or a clanging bell. [2] I may have the gift of inspired preaching; I may have all knowledge and understand all secrets; I may have all the faith needed to move mountains—but if I have no love, I am nothing. [3] I may give away everything I have, and even give up my body to be burned[n]—but if I have no love, this does me no good.

[4] Love is patient and kind; it is not jealous or conceited or proud; [5] love is not ill-mannered or selfish or irritable; love does not keep a record of wrongs; [6] love is not happy with evil, but is happy with the truth. [7] Love never gives up; and its faith, hope, and patience never fail.

Sharing Each Other's Suffering

2 CORINTHIANS 1:3–7

[3] Let us give thanks to the God and Father of our Lord Jesus Christ, the merciful Father, the God from whom all help comes! [4] He helps us in all our troubles, so that we are able to help others who have all kinds of troubles, using the same help that we ourselves have received from God. [5] Just as we have a share in Christ's many sufferings, so also through Christ we share in God's great

help. ⁶ If we suffer, it is for your help and salvation; if we are helped, then you too are helped and given the strength to endure with patience the same sufferings that we also endure. ⁷ So our hope in you is never shaken; we know that just as you share in our sufferings, you also share in the help we receive.

2 CORINTHIANS 11:27–29

²⁷ There has been work and toil; often I have gone without sleep; I have been hungry and thirsty; I have often been without enough food, shelter, or clothing. ²⁸ And not to mention other things, every day I am under the pressure of my concern for all the churches. ²⁹ When someone is weak, then I feel weak too; when someone is led into sin, I am filled with distress.

Do Good to Everyone

GALATIANS 6:9–10

⁹ So let us not become tired of doing good; for if we do not give up, the time will come when we will reap the harvest.   So then, as often as we have the chance, we should do good to everyone, and especially to those who belong to our family in the faith.

Widows

1 TIMOTHY 5:9–10

⁹ Do not add any widow to the list of widows unless she is over sixty years of age. In addition, she must have been married only once[h] ¹⁰ and have a reputation for good deeds: a woman who brought up her children well, received strangers in her home, performed humble duties for fellow Christians, helped people in trouble, and devoted herself to doing good.

Keep On Loving One Another

HEBREWS 13:1–3

Keep on loving one another as Christian brothers. [2] Remember to welcome strangers in your homes. There were some who did that and welcomed angels without knowing it. [3] Remember those who are in prison, as though you were in prison with them. Remember those who are suffering, as though you were suffering as they are.

How To Treat Rich and Poor

JAMES 2:1–9

My brothers, as believers in our Lord Jesus Christ, the Lord of glory, you must never treat people in different ways according to their outward appearance. [2] Suppose a rich man wearing a gold ring and fine clothes comes to your meeting, and a poor man in ragged clothes also comes. [3] If you show more respect to the well-dressed man and say to him, "Have this best seat here," but say to the poor man, "Stand over there, or sit here on the floor by my feet," [4] then you are guilty of creating distinctions among yourselves and of making judgments based on evil motives.

[5] Listen, my dear brothers! God chose the poor people of this world to be rich in faith and to possess the kingdom which he promised to those who love him. [6] But you dishonor the poor! Who are the ones who oppress you and drag you before the judges? The rich! [7] They are the ones who speak evil of that good name which has been given to you.

[8] You will be doing the right thing if you obey the law of the Kingdom, which is found in the scripture. "Love your neighbor as you love yourself." [9] But if you treat people according to their outward appearance, you are guilty of sin, and the Law condemns you as a lawbreaker.

IV

PROPERTY AND POSSESSIONS

CREATION IS GOOD

Thanksgiving for Creation

1 TIMOTHY 4:4–5

⁴ Everything that God has created is good; nothing is to be rejected, but everything is to be received with a prayer of thanks, ⁵ because the word of God and the prayer make it acceptable to God.

God Was Pleased

GENESIS 1:11–12; 20–25

¹¹ Then he commanded, "Let the earth produce all kinds of plants, those that bear grain and those that bear fruit"—and it was done. ¹² So the earth produced all kinds of plants, and God was pleased with what he saw . . .

²⁰ Then God commanded, "Let the water be filled with many kinds of living beings, and let the air be filled with birds." ²¹ So God created the great sea monsters, all kinds of creatures that live in the water, and all kinds of birds. And God was pleased with what he saw. ²² He blessed them all and told the creatures that live in the water to reproduce and to fill the sea, and he told the birds to increase in number . . .

²⁴ Then God commanded, "Let the earth produce all kinds of animal life: domestic and wild, large and small"—and it was done. ²⁵ So God made them all, and he was pleased with what he saw.

PSALM 65:9–13

⁹ You show your care for the land by sending rain;
　　you make it rich and fertile.
　You fill the streams with water;
　　you provide the earth with crops.
　This is how you do it:
¹⁰　you send abundant rain on the plowed fields
　　and soak them with water;
　you soften the soil with showers
　　and cause the young plants to grow.
¹¹ What a rich harvest your goodness provides!
　　Wherever you go there is plenty.
¹² The pastures are filled with flocks;
　　the hillsides are full of joy.
¹³ The fields are covered with sheep;
　　the valleys are full of wheat.
　Everything shouts and sings for joy.

PSALM 144:12–15

¹² May our sons in their youth be like plants that grow up
　　　strong.
　May our daughters be like stately columns
　　which adorn the corners of a palace.
¹³ May our barns be filled with crops of every kind.
　May the sheep in our fields
　　bear young by the tens of thousands.
¹⁴ May our cattle reproduce plentifully
　　without miscarriage or loss.
　May there be no cries of distress in our streets.
¹⁵ Happy is the nation of whom this is true;
　　happy are the people whose God is the LORD!

PSALM 145:15–16

¹⁵ All living things look hopefully to you,
　　and you give them food when they need it.
¹⁶ You give them enough and satisfy the needs of all.

⁷ Go ahead—eat your food and be happy; drink your wine and be cheerful. It's all right with God.

God Prepares a Banquet

ISAIAH 25:6-8

⁶ Here on Mount Zion the LORD Almighty will prepare a banquet for all the nations of the world—a banquet of the richest food and the finest wine. ⁷ Here he will suddenly remove the cloud of sorrow that has been hanging over all the nations. ⁸ The Sovereign LORD will destroy death forever! He will wipe away the tears from everyone's eyes and take away the disgrace his people have suffered throughout the world. The LORD himself has spoken.

The New Heaven and the New Earth

REVELATION 21:1-5; 22-27

Then I saw a new heaven and a new earth. The first heaven and the first earth disappeared, and the sea vanished. ² And I saw the Holy City, the new Jerusalem, coming down out of heaven from God, prepared and ready, like a bride dressed to meet her husband. ³ I heard a loud voice speaking from the throne: "Now God's home is with mankind! He will live with them, and they shall be his people. God himself will be with them, and he will be their God. ⁴ He will wipe away all tears from their eyes. There will be no more death, no more grief or crying or pain. The old things have disappeared."

⁵ Then the one who sits on the throne said, "And now I make all things new!"

²² I did not see a temple in the city because its temple is the Lord God Almighty and the Lamb. ²³ The city has no need of the sun or the moon to shine on it, because the glory of God shines on it, and the Lamb is its lamp. ²⁴ The peoples of the world will walk by its light, and the

kings of the earth will bring their wealth into it. ²⁵ The
gates of the city will stand open all day; they will never be
closed, because there will be no night there. ²⁶ The greatness and the wealth of the nations will be brought into
the city. ²⁷ But nothing that is impure will enter the city,
nor anyone who does shameful things or tells lies. Only
those whose names are written in the Lamb's book of the
living will enter the city.

—NECESSITIES FOR EVERYONE—

How To Pray

MATTHEW 6:9–13

⁹ This, then, is how you should pray:
> 'Our Father in heaven:
> May your holy name be honored;
>
> ¹⁰   may your Kingdom come;
>   may your will be done on earth as it is in
>   heaven.
>
> ¹¹   Give us today the food we need.
>
> ¹²   Forgive us the wrongs we have done,
>   as we forgive the wrongs that others have
>   done to us.
>
> ¹³   Do not bring us to hard testing,
>   but keep us safe from the Evil One.'

God's Promise

GENESIS 8:15–22

¹⁵ God said to Noah, ¹⁶ "Go out of the boat with
your wife, your sons, and their wives. ¹⁷ Take all the birds
and animals out with you, so that they may reproduce
and spread over all the earth." ¹⁸ So Noah went out of the
boat with his wife, his sons, and their wives. ¹⁹ All the
animals and birds went out of the boat in groups of their
own kind.

[20] Noah built an altar to the LORD; he took one of each kind of ritually clean animal and bird, and burned them whole as a sacrifice on the altar. [21] The odor of the sacrifice pleased the LORD, and he said to himself, "Never again will I put the earth under a curse because of what man does; I know that from the time he is young his thoughts are evil. Never again will I destroy all living beings, as I have done this time. [22] As long as the world exists, there will be a time for planting and a time for harvest. There will always be cold and heat, summer and winter, day and night."

The Manna and the Quails

EXODUS 16:1–36

The whole Israelite community set out from Elim, and on the fifteenth day of the second month after they had left Egypt, they came to the desert of Sin, which is between Elim and Sinai. [2] There in the desert they all complained to Moses and Aaron [3] and said to them, "We wish that the LORD had killed us in Egypt. There we could at least sit down and eat meat and as much other food as we wanted. But you have brought us out into this desert to starve us all to death."

[4] The LORD said to Moses, "Now I am going to cause food to rain down from the sky for all of you. The people must go out every day and gather enough for that day. In this way I can test them to find out if they will follow my instructions. [5] On the sixth day they are to bring in twice as much as usual and prepare it."

[6] So Moses and Aaron said to all the Israelites, "This evening you will know that it was the LORD who brought you out of Egypt. [7] In the morning you will see the dazzling light of the LORD's presence. He has heard your complaints against him—yes, against him, because we are only carrying out his instructions." [8] Then Moses said, "It is the LORD who will give you meat to eat in the evening and as much bread as you want in the morning, be-

cause he has heard how much you have complained against him. When you complain against us, you are really complaining against the LORD."

⁹ Moses said to Aaron, "Tell the whole community to come and stand before the LORD, because he has heard their complaints." ¹⁰ As Aaron spoke to the whole community, they turned toward the desert, and suddenly the dazzling light of the LORD appeared in a cloud. ¹¹ The LORD said to Moses, ¹² "I have heard the complaints of the Israelites. Tell them that at twilight they will have meat to eat, and in the morning they will have all the bread they want. Then they will know that I, the LORD, am their God."

¹³ In the evening a large flock of quails flew in, enough to cover the camp, and in the morning there was dew all around the camp. ¹⁴ When the dew evaporated, there was something thin and flaky on the surface of the desert. It was as delicate as frost. ¹⁵ When the Israelites saw it, they didn't know what it was and asked each other, "What is it?"

Moses said to them, "This is the food that the LORD has given you to eat. ¹⁶ The LORD has commanded that each of you is to gather as much of it as he needs, two quarts for each member of his household."

¹⁷ The Israelites did this, some gathering more, others less. ¹⁸ When they measured it, those who had gathered more did not have too much, and those who had gathered less did not have too little. Each had gathered just what he needed. ¹⁹ Moses said to them, "No one is to keep any of it for tomorrow." ²⁰ But some of them did not listen to Moses and saved part of it. The next morning it was full of worms and smelled rotten, and Moses was angry with them. ²¹ Every morning each one gathered as much as he needed; and when the sun grew hot, what was left on the ground melted.

²² On the sixth day they gathered twice as much food, four quarts for each person. All the leaders of the community came and told Moses about it, ²³ and he said

to them, "The LORD has commanded that tomorrow is a holy day of rest, dedicated to him. Bake today what you want to bake and boil what you want to boil. Whatever is left should be put aside and kept for tomorrow." [24] As Moses had commanded, they kept what was left until the next day; it did not spoil or get worms in it. [25] Moses said, "Eat this today, because today is the Sabbath, a day of rest dedicated to the LORD, and you will not find any food outside the camp. [26] You must gather food for six days, but on the seventh day, the day of rest, there will be none."

[27] On the seventh day some of the people went out to gather food, but they did not find any. [28] Then the LORD said to Moses, "How much longer will you people refuse to obey my commands? [29] Remember that I, the LORD, have given you a day of rest, and that is why on the sixth day I will always give you enough food for two days. Everyone is to stay where he is on the seventh day and not leave his home." [30] So the people did not work on the seventh day.

[31] The people of Israel called the food manna.° It was like a small white seed, and tasted like thin cakes made with honey. [32] Moses said, "The LORD has commanded us to save some manna, to be kept for our descendants, so that they can see the food which he gave us to eat in the desert when he brought us out of Egypt." [33] Moses said to Aaron, "Take a jar, put two quarts of manna in it, and place it in the LORD's presence to be kept for our descendants." [34] As the LORD had commanded Moses, Aaron put it in front of the Covenant Box, so that it could be kept. [35] The Israelites ate manna for the next forty years, until they reached the land of Canaan, where they settled. ([36] The standard dry measure then in use equaled twenty quarts.)

Water from the Rock

EXODUS 17:1–7

The whole Israelite community left the desert of Sin, moving from one place to another at the command of the LORD. They camped at Rephidim, but there was no water there to drink. ² They complained to Moses and said, "Give us water to drink."

Moses answered, "Why are you complaining? Why are you putting the LORD to the test?"

³ But the people were very thirsty and continued to complain to Moses. They said, "Why did you bring us out of Egypt? To kill us and our children and our livestock with thirst?"

⁴ Moses prayed earnestly to the LORD and said, "What can I do with these people? They are almost ready to stone me."

⁵ The LORD said to Moses, "Take some of the leaders of Israel with you, and go on ahead of the people. Take along the stick with which you struck the Nile. ⁶ I will stand before you on a rock at Mount Sinai. Strike the rock, and water will come out of it for the people to drink." Moses did so in the presence of the leaders of Israel.

⁷ The place was named Massah and Meribah,ᵖ because the Israelites complained and put the LORD to the test when they asked, "Is the LORD with us or not?"

The Lord Gives Life

ISAIAH 55:1–3

The LORD says,
"Come, everyone who is thirsty—
here is water!
Come, you that have no money—
buy grain and eat!
Come! Buy wine and milk—
it will cost you nothing!

² Why spend money on what does not satisfy?
   Why spend your wages and still be hungry?
Listen to me and do what I say
   and you will enjoy the best food of all.

³ "Listen now, my people, and come to me;
   come to me, and you will have life!
I will make a lasting covenant with you
   and give you the blessings I promised to David.

A Drink of Water

MATTHEW 10:42

⁴² "You can be sure that whoever gives even a drink of cold water to one of the least of these my followers because he is my follower, will certainly receive a reward."

Lord of the Sabbath

MATTHEW 12:1–8

Not long afterward Jesus was walking through some wheat fields on a Sabbath. His disciples were hungry, so they began to pick heads of wheat and eat the grain. ² When the Pharisees saw this, they said to Jesus, "Look, it is against our Law for your disciples to do this on the Sabbath!"

³ Jesus answered, "Have you never read what David did that time when he and his men were hungry? ⁴ He went into the house of God, and he and his men ate the bread offered to God, even though it was against the Law for them to eat it—only the priests were allowed to eat that bread. ⁵ Or have you not read in the Law of Moses that every Sabbath the priests in the Temple actually break the Sabbath law, yet they are not guilty? ⁶ I tell you that there is something here greater than the Temple. ⁷ The scripture says, 'It is kindness that I want, not animal sacrifices.' If you really knew what this means, you

would not condemn people who are not guilty; ⁸for the Son of Man is Lord of the Sabbath."

Jesus Feeds Four Thousand People

MARK 8:1–9

Not long afterward another large crowd came together. When the people had nothing left to eat, Jesus called the disciples to him and said, ² "I feel sorry for these people, because they have been with me for three days and now have nothing to eat. ³ If I send them home without feeding them, they will faint as they go, because some of them have come a long way."

⁴ His disciples asked him, "Where in this desert can anyone find enough food to feed all these people?"

⁵ "How much bread do you have?" Jesus asked.

"Seven loaves," they answered.

⁶ He ordered the crowd to sit down on the ground. Then he took the seven loaves, gave thanks to God, broke them, and gave them to his disciples to distribute to the crowd; and the disciples did so. ⁷ They also had a few small fish. Jesus gave thanks for these and told the disciples to distribute them too. ⁸⁻⁹ Everybody ate and had enough—there were about four thousand people. Then the disciples took up seven baskets full of pieces left over.

Never Again Will They Hunger

REVELATION 7:13–17

¹³ One of the elders asked me, "Who are these people dressed in white robes, and where do they come from?"

¹⁴ "I don't know, sir. You do." I answered.

He said to me, "These are the people who have come safely through the terrible persecution. They have washed their robes and made them white with the blood of the Lamb. ¹⁵ That is why they stand before God's throne and serve him day and night in his temple. He

121

who sits on the throne will protect them with his presence. ¹⁶ Never again will they hunger or thirst; neither sun nor any scorching heat will burn them, ¹⁷ because the Lamb, who is in the center of the throne, will be their shepherd, and he will guide them to springs of life-giving water. And God will wipe away every tear from their eyes."

WHO OWNS THE WORLD?

The Earth Is the Lord's

DEUTERONOMY 10:14
   ¹⁴ To the Lord belong even the highest heavens; the earth is his also, and everything on it.

PSALM 24:1
   The world and all that is in it belong to the LORD;
      the earth and all who live on it are his.

EXODUS 19:5
   ⁵ Now, if you will obey me and keep my covenant, you will be my own people. The whole earth is mine, but you will be my chosen people.

The Ten Commandments

EXODUS 20:1–3; 13; 15; 17
   God spoke, and these were his words: ² "I am the LORD your God who brought you out of Egypt, where you were slaves.
   ³ "Worship no god but me.
   ¹³ "Do not commit murder.
   ¹⁵ "Do not steal.

¹⁷ "Do not desire another man's house; do not desire his wife, his slaves, his cattle, his donkeys, or anything else that he owns."

God's Gift

1 CHRONICLES 29:10–14

¹⁰ There in front of the whole assembly King David praised the LORD. He said, "LORD God of our ancestor Jacob, may you be praised forever and ever! ¹¹ You are great and powerful, glorious, splendid, and majestic. Everything in heaven and earth is yours, and you are king, supreme ruler over all. ¹² All riches and wealth come from you; you rule everything by your strength and power; and you are able to make anyone great and strong. ¹³ Now, our God, we give you thanks, and we praise your glorious name.

¹⁴ "Yet my people and I cannot really give you anything, because everything is a gift from you, and we have only given back what is yours already.

PSALM 50:10–12

¹⁰ All the animals in the forest are mine
    and the cattle on thousands of hills.
¹¹ All the wild birds are mine
    and all living things in the fields.

¹² "If I were hungry, I would not tell you,
    for the world and everything in it is mine.

PSALM 82:8

⁸ Come, O God, and rule the world;
    all the nations are yours.

ECCLESIASTES 3:13

¹³ All of us should eat and drink and enjoy what we have worked for. It is God's gift.

A CAREFREE ATTITUDE TOWARD
POSSESSIONS

Do Not Love the World

1 JOHN 2:15–17

¹⁵ Do not love the world or anything that belongs to the world. If you love the world, you do not love the Father. ¹⁶ Everything that belongs to the world—what the sinful self desires, what people see and want, and everything in this world that people are so proud of—none of this comes from the Father; it all comes from the world. ¹⁷ The world and everything in it that people desire is passing away; but he who does the will of God lives forever.

PSALM 37:16

¹⁶ The little that a good man owns
   is worth more than the wealth
      of all the wicked,

No Escape from Death

PSALM 49:5–14; 16–20

⁵ I am not afraid in times of danger
   when I am surrounded by enemies,
⁶ by evil men who trust in their riches
   and boast of their great wealth.
⁷ A person can never redeem himself;
   he cannot pay God the price for his life,
⁸ because the payment for a human life is too great.
   What he could pay would never be enough
⁹ to keep him from the grave,
   to let him live forever.

[10] Anyone can see that even wise men die,
as well as foolish and stupid men.
They all leave their riches to their descendants.
[11] Their graves are their homes forever;
there they stay for all time,
though they once had lands of their own.

[12] A man's greatness cannot keep him from death;
he will still die like the animals.

[13] See what happens to those who trust in themselves,
the fate of those who are satisfied with their wealth—
[14] they are doomed to die like sheep,
and Death will be their shepherd.
[16] Don't be upset when a man becomes rich,
when his wealth grows even greater;
[17] he cannot take it with him when he dies;
his wealth will not go with him to the grave.
[18] Even if a man is satisfied with this life
and is praised because he is successful,
[19] he will join all his ancestors in death,
where the darkness lasts forever.
[20] A man's greatness cannot keep him from death;
he will still die like the animals.

More Valuable Than Riches

PSALM 119:36–37
[36] Give me the desire to obey your laws
rather than to get rich.
[37] Keep me from paying attention to what is worthless;
be good to me, as you have promised.

PROVERBS 11:7
[7] When a wicked man dies, his hope dies with him.
Confidence placed in riches comes to nothing.

PROVERBS 15:16–17

¹⁶ Better to be poor and fear the LORD than to be rich and in trouble.

¹⁷ Better to eat vegetables with people you love than to eat the finest meat where there is hate.

PROVERBS 16:16; 19

¹⁶ It is better—much better—to have wisdom and knowledge than gold and silver.

¹⁹ It is better to be humble and stay poor than to be one of the arrogant and get a share of their loot.

PROVERBS 19:1

It is better to be poor but honest than to be a lying fool.

PROVERBS 22:1

If you have to choose between a good reputation and great wealth, choose a good reputation.

PROVERBS 23:4–8

⁴ Be wise enough not to wear yourself out trying to get rich. ⁵ Your money can be gone in a flash, as if it had grown wings and flown away like an eagle.

⁶ Don't eat at the table of a stingy man or be greedy for the fine food he serves. ⁷ "Come on and have some more," he says, but he doesn't mean it. What he thinks is what he really is. ⁸ You will vomit up what you have eaten, and all your flattery will be wasted.

PROVERBS 28:6

⁶ Better to be poor and honest than rich and dishonest.

Useless Work

ECCLESIASTES 4:4–8; 13–14

⁴ I have also learned why people work so hard to succeed: it is because they envy the things their neighbors have. But it is useless. It is like chasing the wind. ⁵ They say that a man would be a fool to fold his hands and let himself starve to death. ⁶ Maybe so, but it is better to have only a little, with peace of mind, than be busy all the time with both hands, trying to catch the wind.

⁷ I have noticed something else in life that is useless. ⁸ Here is a man who lives alone. He has no son, no brother, yet he is always working, never satisfied with the wealth he has. For whom is he working so hard and denying himself any pleasure? This is useless, too—and a miserable way to live.

¹³⁻¹⁴ A man may rise from poverty to become king of his country, or go from prison to the throne, but if in his old age he is too foolish to take advice, he is not as well off as a young man who is poor but intelligent.

On Borrowing

MATTHEW 5:42

⁴² When someone asks you for something, give it to him; when someone wants to borrow something, lend it to him.

On Storing Up Riches

MATTHEW 6:19–21

¹⁹ "Do not store up riches for yourselves here on earth, where moths and rust destroy, and robbers break in and steal. ²⁰ Instead, store up riches for yourselves in heaven, where moths and rust cannot destroy, and robbers cannot break in and steal. ²¹ For your heart will always be where your riches are.

This text demands a basic choice in our values, goals and direction in life. The language is strong. The verb "serve" in verse 24 takes on particularly potent meaning because of the reference to slavery earlier in the same verse. We must choose either bondage to God or bondage to possessions.

Jesus then proceeds to explain the paradoxical fact that when we stop seeking security in earthly things and seek security only in our Father, we discover a new freedom from the anxieties that plague the rest of the world (v. 32). We are to learn from the wild grass of the field. In Palestine, grass did not live long because of the hot south wind (it was also used as fuel in ovens). In spite of this transience, the grass is nevertheless wonderfully clothed by the Father and enveloped by his care. Surely, Jesus implies, the Father cares far more for each of us.

For further study: *in addition to BB, IB, ICC, NBC, and NCC, see also Eduard Schweitzer,* The Good News According to Matthew, *trans. David E. Green (Atlanta: The John Knox Press, 1975); R. V. G. Tasker,* The Gospel According to St. Matthew *(TNT, Grand Rapids: Eerdmans Pub. Co., 1961).*

God and Possessions

MATTHEW 6:24–33

²⁴ "No one can be a slave of two masters; he will hate one and love the other; he will be loyal to one and despise the other. You cannot serve both God and money.

²⁵ "This is why I tell you: do not be worried about the food and drink you need in order to stay alive, or about clothes for your body. After all, isn't life worth more than food? And isn't the body worth more than clothes? ²⁶ Look at the birds flying around: they do not plant seeds, gather a harvest and put it in barns; yet the Father in heaven takes care of them! Aren't you worth

much more than birds? ²⁷ Can any of you live a bit lon-gerᵈ by worrying about it?

²⁸ "And why worry about clothes? Look how the wild flowers grow: they do not work or make clothes for themselves. ²⁹ But I tell you that not even King Solomon with all his wealth had clothes as beautiful as one of these flowers. ³⁰ It is God who clothes the wild grass—grass that is here today and gone tomorrow, burned up in the oven. Won't he be all the more sure to clothe you? What little faith you have!

³¹ "So do not start worrying: 'Where will my food come from? or my drink? or my clothes?' ³² (These are the things the pagans are always concerned about.) Your Father in heaven knows that you need all these things. ³³ Instead, be concerned above everything else with the Kingdom of God and with what he requires of you, and he will provide you with all these other things.

Giving and Receiving

ACTS 20:32–35

³² "And now I commend you to the care of God and to the message of his grace, which is able to build you up and give you the blessings God has for all his people. ³³ I have not wanted anyone's silver or gold or clothing. ³⁴ You yourselves know that I have worked with these hands of mine to provide everything that my companions and I have needed. ³⁵ I have shown you in all things that by working hard in this way we must help the weak, re-membering the words that the Lord Jesus himself said, 'There is more happiness in giving than in receiving.' "

Having Nothing and Possessing Everything

2 CORINTHIANS 6:5; 8–10

⁵ We have been beaten, jailed, and mobbed; we have been overworked and have gone without sleep or food.

⁸ We are honored and disgraced; we are insulted and praised. We are treated as liars, yet we speak the truth; ⁹ as unknown, yet we are known by all; as though we were dead, but, as you see, we live on. Although punished, we are not killed; ¹⁰ although saddened, we are always glad; we seem poor, but we make many people rich; we seem to have nothing, yet we really possess everything.

Learn to Be Content

PHILIPPIANS 4:11–13
¹¹ I have learned to be satisfied with what I have. ¹² I know what it is to be in need and what it is to have more than enough. I have learned this secret, so that anywhere, at any time, I am content, whether I am full or hungry, whether I have too much or too little. ¹³ I have the strength to face all conditions by the power that Christ gives me.

Church Leaders and Money

1 TIMOTHY 3:2–3
² A church leader must be without fault; he must have only one wife,ᶜ be sober, self-controlled, and orderly; he must welcome strangers in his home; he must be able to teach; ³ he must not be a drunkard or a violent man, but gentle and peaceful; he must not love money.

A Lasting Possession

HEBREWS 10:32–34
³² Remember how it was with you in the past. In those days, after God's light had shone on you, you suffered many things, yet were not defeated by the struggle. ³³ You were at times publicly insulted and mistreated, and at other times you were ready to join those who were being treated in this way. ³⁴ You shared the sufferings of

prisoners, and when all your belongings were seized, you endured your loss gladly, because you knew that you still possessed something much better, which would last forever.

Be Satisfied

HEBREWS 13:5
⁵ Keep your lives free from the love of money, and be satisfied with what you have. For God has said, "I will never leave you; I will never abandon you."

JAMES 1:9–11
⁹ The Christian who is poor must be glad when God lifts him up, ¹⁰ and the rich Christian must be glad when God brings him down. For the rich will pass away like the flower of a wild plant. ¹¹ The sun rises with its blazing heat and burns the plant; its flower falls off, and its beauty is destroyed. In the same way the rich man will be destroyed while he goes about his business.

ARE POSSESSIONS DANGEROUS?

ECCLESIASTES 5:10–12
¹⁰ If you love money, you will never be satisfied; if you long to be rich, you will never get all you want. It is useless. ¹¹ The richer you are, the more mouths you have to feed. All you gain is the knowledge that you are rich. ¹² A working man may or may not have enough to eat, but at least he can get a good night's sleep. A rich man, however, has so much that he stays awake worrying.

PROVERBS 11:28

²⁸ Those who depend on their wealth will fall like the leaves of autumn, but the righteous will prosper like the leaves of summer.

PROVERBS 13:8

⁸ A rich man has to use his money to save his life, but no one threatens a poor man.

PROVERBS 18:10–11

¹⁰ The LORD is like a strong tower, where the righteous can go and be safe. ¹¹ Rich people, however, imagine that their wealth protects them like high, strong walls around a city.

PROVERBS 28:11

¹¹ Rich people always think they are wise, but a poor person who has insight into character knows better.

LUKE 16:14–15

¹⁴ When the Pharisees heard all this, they made fun of Jesus, because they loved money. ¹⁵ Jesus said to them, "You are the ones who make yourselves look right in other people's sight, but God knows your hearts. For the things that are considered of great value by man are worth nothing in God's sight.

Jesus and the Moneychangers

JOHN 2:13–16

¹³ It was almost time for the Passover Festival, so Jesus went to Jerusalem. ¹⁴ There in the Temple he found men selling cattle, sheep, and pigeons, and also the moneychangers sitting at their tables. ¹⁵ So he made a whip from cords and drove all the animals out of the Temple, both the sheep and the cattle; he overturned the tables of the moneychangers and scattered their coins; ¹⁶ and he

ordered the men who sold the pigeons, "Take them out of here! Stop making my Father's house a marketplace!"

Buying God's Gift

ACTS 8:18–24

[18] Simon saw that the Spirit had been given to the believers when the apostles placed their hands on them. So he offered money to Peter and John, [19] and said, "Give this power to me too, so that anyone I place my hands on will receive the Holy Spirit."

[20] But Peter answered him, "May you and your money go to hell, for thinking that you can buy God's gift with money! [21] You have no part or share in our work, because your heart is not right in God's sight. [22] Repent, then, of this evil plan of yours, and pray to the Lord that he will forgive you for thinking such a thing as this. [23] For I see that you are full of bitter envy and are a prisoner of sin."

[24] Simon said to Peter and John, "Please pray to the Lord for me, so that none of these things you spoke of will happen to me."

TITUS 1:10–11

[10] For there are many, especially the converts from Judaism, who rebel and deceive others with their nonsense. [11] It is necessary to stop their talk, because they are upsetting whole families by teaching what they should not, and all for the shameful purpose of making money.

REVELATION 3:14–18

[14] "To the angel of the church in Laodicea write:

[17] You say, 'I am rich and well off; I have all I need.' But you do not know how miserable and pitiful you are! You are poor, naked, and blind. [18] I advise you, then, to buy gold from me, pure gold, in order to be rich.

—THE TEMPTATION TO FORSAKE GOD—

The Trap of Riches

1 TIMOTHY 6:6–10

⁶ Well, religion does make a person very rich, if he is satisfied with what he has. ⁷ What did we bring into the world? Nothing! What can we take out of the world? Nothing! ⁸ So then, if we have food and clothes, that should be enough for us. ⁹ But those who want to get rich fall into temptation and are caught in the trap of many foolish and harmful desires, which pull them down to ruin and destruction. ¹⁰ For the love of money is a source of all kinds of evil. Some have been so eager to have it that they have wandered away from the faith and have broken their hearts with many sorrows.

Complaint of the Israelites

NUMBERS 11:4–20

⁴ There were foreigners traveling with the Israelites. They had a strong craving for meat, and even the Israelites themselves began to complain: "If only we could have some meat! ⁵ In Egypt we used to eat all the fish we wanted, and it cost us nothing. Remember the cucumbers, the watermelons, the leeks, the onions, and the garlic we had? ⁶ But now our strength is gone. There is nothing at all to eat—nothing but this manna day after day!"

(⁷ Manna was like small seeds, whitish yellow in color. ⁸⁻⁹ It fell on the camp at night along with the dew. The next morning the people would go around and gather it, grind it or pound it into flour, and then boil it and make it into flat cakes. It tasted like bread baked with olive oil.)

¹⁰ Moses heard all the people complaining as they stood around in groups at the entrances of their tents. He was distressed because the LORD had become angry with them, ¹¹ and he said to the LORD, "Why have you treated

me so badly? Why are you displeased with me? Why have you given me the responsibility for all these people? ^{12} I didn't create them or bring them to birth! Why should you ask me to act like a nurse and carry them in my arms like babies all the way to the land you promised to their ancestors? ^{13}Where could I get enough meat for all these people? They keep whining and asking for meat. ^{14} I can't be responsible for all these people by myself; it's too much for me! ^{15} If you are going to treat me like this, have pity on me and kill me, so that I won't have to endure your cruelty any longer."

^{16} The LORD said to Moses. "Assemble seventy respected men who are recognized as leaders of the people, bring them to me at the Tent of my presence, and tell them to stand there beside you. ^{17} I will come down and speak with you there, and I will take some of the spirit I have given you and give it to them. Then they can help you bear the responsibility for these people, and you will not have to bear it alone. ^{18} Now tell the people, 'Purify yourselves for tomorrow; you will have meat to eat. The LORD has heard you whining and saying that you wished you had some meat and that you were better off in Egypt. Now the LORD will give you meat, and you will have to eat it. ^{19} You will have to eat it not just for one or two days, or five, or ten, or even twenty days, ^{20} but for a whole month, until it comes out of your ears, until you are sick of it. This will happen because you have rejected the LORD who is here among you and have complained to him that you should never have left Egypt.' "

NUMBERS 21:4–9

^{4} The Israelites left Mount Hor by the road that leads to the Gulf of Aqaba, in order to go around the territory of Edom. But on the way the people lost their patience ^{5} and spoke against God and Moses. They complained, "Why did you bring us out of Egypt to die in this desert, where there is no food or water? We can't stand any more of this miserable food!" ^{6} Then the LORD sent poisonous snakes among the people, and many Israelites were bitten and died. [7] The people came to Moses and said, "We sinned when we spoke against the LORD and against you. Now pray to the LORD to take these snakes away." So Moses prayed for the people. [8] Then the LORD told Moses to make a metal snake and put it on a pole, so that anyone who was bitten could look at it and be healed. [9] So Moses made a bronze snake and put it on a pole. Anyone who had been bitten would look at the bronze snake and be healed.

Do Not Forget the Lord

DEUTERONOMY 6:4–12

[4] "Israel, remember this! The LORD—and the LORD alone—is our God.[f] [5] Love the LORD your God with all your heart, with all your soul, and with all your strength. [6] Never forget these commands that I am giving you today. [7] Teach them to your children. Repeat them when you are at home and when you are away, when you are resting and when you are working. [8] Tie them on your arms and wear them on your foreheads as a reminder. [9] Write them on the doorposts of your houses and on your gates.

[10] "Just as the LORD your God promised your ancestors, Abraham, Isaac, and Jacob, he will give you a land with large and prosperous cities which you did not build. [11] The houses will be full of good things which you did not put in them, and there will be wells that you did not dig, and vineyards and olive orchards that you did not plant. When the LORD brings you into this land and you have all you want to eat, [12] make certain that you do not forget the LORD who rescued you from Egypt, where you were slaves.

A Warning Against Forgetting

"Obey faithfully all the laws that I have given you today, so that you may live, increase in number, and occupy the land that the LORD promised to your ancestors. ² Remember how the LORD your God led you on this long journey through the desert these past forty years, sending hardships to test you, so that he might know what you intended to do and whether you would obey his commands. ³ He made you go hungry, and then he gave you manna to eat, food that you and your ancestors had never eaten before. He did this to teach you that man must not depend on bread alone to sustain him, but on everything that the LORD says. ⁴ During these forty years your clothes have not worn out, nor have your feet swollen up. ⁵ Remember that the LORD your God corrects and punishes you just as a father disciplines his children. ⁶ So then, do as the LORD has commanded you: live according to his laws and have reverence for him. ⁷ The LORD your God is bringing you into a fertile land—a land that has rivers and springs, and underground streams gushing out into the valleys and hills; ⁸ a land that produces wheat and barley, grapes, figs, pomegranates, olives, and honey.

⁹ "There you will never go hungry or ever be in need. Its rocks have iron in them, and from its hills you can mine copper. ¹⁰ You will have all you want to eat, and you will give thanks to the LORD your God for the fertile land that he has given you.

¹¹ "Make certain that you do not forget the LORD your God; do not fail to obey any of his laws that I am giving you today. ¹² When you have all you want to eat and have built good houses to live in ¹³ and when your cattle and sheep, your silver and gold, and all your other possessions have increased, ¹⁴ be sure that you do not become proud and forget the LORD your God who rescued you from Egypt, where you were slaves. ¹⁵ He led you

137

through that vast and terrifying desert where there were poisonous snakes and scorpions. In that dry and waterless land he made water flow out of solid rock for you. [16] In the desert he gave you manna to eat, food that your ancestors had never eaten. He sent hardships on you to test you, so that in the end he could bless you with good things. [17] So then, you must never think that you have made yourselves wealthy by your own power and strength. [18] Remember that it is the LORD your God who gives you the power to become rich. He does this because he is still faithful today to the covenant that he made with your ancestors. [19] Never forget the LORD your God or turn to other gods to worship and serve them. If you do, then I warn you today that you will certainly be destroyed. [20] If you do not obey the LORD, then you will be destroyed just like those nations that he is going to destroy as you advance.

Abandoning God

DEUTERONOMY 32:15
[15] "The LORD's people grew rich, but rebellious;
    they were fat and stuffed with food.
  They abandoned God their Creator
    and rejected their mighty savior.

PROVERBS 30:8–9
[8] Keep me from lying, and let me be neither rich nor poor. So give me only as much food as I need. [9] If I have more, I might say that I do not need you. But if I am poor, I might steal and bring disgrace on my God.

EZEKIEL 7:20
Gold and silver led them into sin. [20] Once they were proud of their beautiful jewels, but they used them to make disgusting idols. That is why the LORD has made their wealth repulsive to them.

138

¹ The people of Israel were like a grapevine that was full of grapes. The more prosperous they were, the more altars they built. The more productive their land was, the more beautiful they made the sacred stone pillars they worship. ² The people whose hearts are deceitful must now suffer for their sins. God will break down their altars and destroy their sacred pillars.

⁴ The LORD says, "I am the LORD your God, who led you out of Egypt. You have no God but me. I alone am your savior. ⁵ I took care of you in a dry, desert land. ⁶ But when you entered the good land, you became full and satisfied, and then you grew proud and forgot me. ⁷ So I will attack you like a lion. Like a leopard I will lie in wait along your path. ⁸ I will attack you like a bear that has lost her cubs, and I will tear you open. Like a lion I will devour you on the spot, and will tear you to pieces like a wild animal.

The Temptation of Jesus

Then the Spirit led Jesus into the desert to be tempted by the Devil. ² After spending forty days and nights without food, Jesus was hungry. ³ Then the Devil came to him and said, "If you are God's Son, order these stones to turn into bread."

⁴ But Jesus answered, "The scripture says, 'Man cannot live on bread alone, but needs every word that God speaks.' "

⁸ Then the Devil took Jesus to a very high mountain and showed him all the kingdoms of the world in all their greatness. ⁹ "All this I will give you," the Devil said, "if you kneel down and worship me."

¹⁰ Then Jesus answered, "Go away, Satan! The scrip-

ture says, 'Worship the Lord your God and serve only him!' "

Choking the Message

MATTHEW **13:22**

²² The seeds that fell among thorn bushes stand for those who hear the message; but the worries about this life and the love for riches choke the message, and they don't bear fruit.

The Rich Young Man

MATTHEW **19:16–30**

¹⁶ Once a man came to Jesus, "Teacher," he asked, "what good thing must I do to receive eternal life?"

¹⁷ "Why do you ask me concerning what is good?" answered Jesus. "There is only One who is good. Keep the commandments if you want to enter life."

¹⁸ "What commandments?" he asked.

Jesus answered, "Do not commit murder; do not commit adultery; do not steal; do not accuse anyone falsely; ¹⁹ respect your father and your mother; and love your neighbor as you love yourself."

²⁰ "I have obeyed all these commandments," the young man replied. "What else do I need to do?"

²¹ Jesus said to him, "If you want to be perfect, go and sell all you have and give the money to the poor, and you will have riches in heaven; then come and follow me."

²² When the young man heard this, he went away sad, because he was very rich.

²³ Jesus then said to his disciples, "I assure you: it will be very hard for rich people to enter the Kingdom of heaven. ²⁴ I repeat: it is much harder for a rich person to enter the Kingdom of God than for a camel to go through the eye of a needle."

²⁵ When the disciples heard this, they were completely amazed. "Who, then, can be saved?" they asked.

²⁶ Jesus looked straight at them and answered, "This is impossible for man, but for God everything is possible."

²⁷ Then Peter spoke up. "Look," he said, "we have left everything and followed you. What will we have?"

²⁸ Jesus said to them, "You can be sure that when the Son of Man sits on his glorious throne in the New Age, then you twelve followers of mine will also sit on thrones, to rule the twelve tribes of Israel. ²⁹ And everyone who has left houses or brothers or sisters or father or mother or children or fields for my sake, will receive a hundred times more and will be given eternal life. ³⁰ But many who now are first will be last, and many who now are last will be first.

The Parable of the Great Feast

LUKE 14:15–23

¹⁵ When one of the men sitting at the table heard this, he said to Jesus, "How happy are those who will sit down at the feast in the Kingdom of God!"

¹⁶ Jesus said to him, "There was once a man who was giving a great feast to which he invited many people. ¹⁷ When it was time for the feast, he sent his servant to tell his guests, 'Come, everything is ready!' ¹⁸ But they all began, one after another, to make excuses. The first one told the servant, 'I have bought a field and must go and look at it; please accept my apologies.' ¹⁹ Another one said, 'I have bought five pairs of oxen and am on my way to try them out; please accept my apologies.' ²⁰ Another one said, 'I have just gotten married, and for that reason I cannot come.' ²¹ The servant went back and told all this to his master. The master was furious and said to his servant, 'Hurry out to the streets and alleys of the town, and bring back the poor, the crippled, the blind, and the

lame.' ²² Soon the servant said, 'Your order has been carried out, sir, but there is room for more.' ²³ So the master said to the servant, 'Go out to the country roads and lanes and make people come in, so that my house will be full.

Testing the Spirit

ACTS 5:1–11

But there was a man named Ananias, who with his wife Sapphira sold some property that belonged to them. ² But with his wife's agreement he kept part of the money for himself and turned the rest over to the apostles. ³ Peter said to him, "Ananias, why did you let Satan take control of you and make you lie to the Holy Spirit by keeping part of the money you received for the property? ⁴ Before you sold the property, it belonged to you; and after you sold it, the money was yours. Why, then, did you decide to do such a thing? You have not lied to men—you have lied to God!" ⁵ As soon as Ananias heard this, he fell down dead; and all who heard about it were terrified. ⁶ The young men came in, wrapped up his body, carried him out, and buried him.

⁷ About three hours later his wife, not knowing what had happened, came in. ⁸ Peter asked her, "Tell me, was this the full amount you and your husband received for your property?"

"Yes," she answered, "the full amount."

⁹ So Peter said to her, "Why did you and your husband decide to put the Lord's Spirit to the test? The men who buried your husband are at the door right now, and they will carry you out too!" ¹⁰ At once she fell down at his feet and died. The young men came in and saw that she was dead, so they carried her out and buried her beside her husband. ¹¹ The whole church and all the others who heard of this were terrified.

Rich in Good Works

1 TIMOTHY 6:17–19

[17] Command those who are rich in the things of this life not to be proud, but to place their hope, not in such an uncertain thing as riches, but in God, who generously gives us everything for our enjoyment. [18] Command them to do good, to be rich in good works, to be generous and ready to share with others. [19] In this way they will store up for themselves a treasure which will be a solid foundation for the future. And then they will be able to win the life which is true life.

For the Sake of Money

JUDE 1:11–12

[11] For the sake of money they have given themselves over to the error that Balaam committed. They have rebelled as Korah rebelled, and like him they are destroyed. [12] With their shameless carousing they are like dirty spots in your fellowship meals.

—GREED—

The Parable of the Rich Fool

LUKE 12:13–21

[13] A man in the crowd said to Jesus, "Teacher, tell my brother to divide with me the property our father left us."

[14] Jesus answered him, "Man, who gave me the right to judge or to divide the property between you two?" [15] And he went on to say to them all, "Watch out and guard yourselves from every kind of greed; because a person's true life is not made up of the things he owns, no matter how rich he may be."

[16] Then Jesus told them this parable: "There was

once a rich man who had land which bore good crops. [17] He began to think to himself, 'I don't have a place to keep all my crops. What can I do? [18] This is what I will do,' he told himself; 'I will tear down my barns and build bigger ones, where I will store the grain and all my other goods. [19] Then I will say to myself, Lucky man! You have all the good things you need for many years. Take life easy, eat, drink, and enjoy yourself!' [20] But God said to him, 'You fool! This very night you will have to give up your life; then who will get all these things you have kept for yourself?' "

[21] And Jesus concluded, "This is how it is with those who pile up riches for themselves but are not rich in God's sight."

The Disgrace of Greed

PROVERBS 19:22
[22] It is a disgrace to be greedy; poor people are better off than liars.

Greed's Ultimate Effect

1 CORINTHIANS 5:11
[11] What I meant was that you should not associate with a person who calls himself a brother but is immoral or greedy or worships idols or is a slanderer or a drunkard or a thief. Don't even sit down to eat with such a person.

1 CORINTHIANS 6:9–10
[9] Surely you know that the wicked will not possess God's Kingdom. Do not fool yourselves; people who are immoral or who worship idols or are adulterers or homosexual perverts [10] or who steal or are greedy or are drunkards or who slander others or are thieves—none of these will possess God's Kingdom.

Greed Is Idolatrous

EPHESIANS 5:3–5

³ Since you are God's people, it is not right that any matters of sexual immorality or indecency or greed should even be mentioned among you. ⁴ Nor is it fitting for you to use language which is obscene, profane, or vulgar. Rather you should give thanks to God. ⁵ You may be sure that no one who is immoral, indecent, or greedy (for greed is a form of idolatry) will ever receive a share in the Kingdom of Christ and of God.

COLOSSIANS 3:5–6

⁵ You must put to death, then, the earthly desires at work in you, such as sexual immorality, indecency, lust, evil passions, and greed (for greed is a form of idolatry). ⁶ Because of such things God's anger will come upon those who do not obey him.ᶜ

Church Helpers

1 TIMOTHY 3:8

⁸ Church helpers must also have a good character and be sincere; they must not drink too much wine or be greedy for money.

Love of Pleasure

2 TIMOTHY 3:1–5

Remember that there will be difficult times in the last days. ² People will be selfish, greedy, boastful, and conceited; they will be insulting, disobedient to their parents, ungrateful, and irreligious; ³ they will be unkind, merciless, slanderers, violent, and fierce; they will hate the good; ⁴ they will be treacherous, reckless, and swollen with pride; they will love pleasure rather than God; ⁵ they will hold to the outward form of our religion, but reject its real power.

A Church Leader

TITUS 1:7

7 For since a church leader is in charge of God's work, he should be without fault. He must not be arrogant or quick-tempered, or a drunkard or violent or greedy for money.

Desire for Pleasure

JAMES 4:1–2

Where do all the fights and quarrels among you come from? They come from your desires for pleasure, which are constantly fighting within you. 2 You want things, but you cannot have them, so you are ready to kill; you strongly desire things, but you cannot get them, so you quarrel and fight.

WHAT ABOUT LAZINESS?

Lazy People

2 THESSALONIANS 3:6–13

6 Our brothers, we command you in the name of our Lord Jesus Christ to keep away from all brothers who are living a lazy life and who do not follow the instructions that we gave them. 7 You yourselves know very well that you should do just what we did. We were not lazy when we were with you. 8 We did not accept anyone's support without paying for it. Instead, we worked and toiled; we kept working day and night so as not to be an expense to any of you. 9 We did this, not because we do not have the right to demand our support; we did it to be an example for you to follow. 10 While we were with you we used to tell you, "Whoever refuses to work is not allowed to eat."

[11] We say this because we hear that there are some people among you who live lazy lives and who do nothing except meddle in other people's business. [12] In the name of the Lord Jesus Christ we command these people and warn them to lead orderly lives and work to earn their own living.

[13] But you, brothers, must not become tired of doing good. [14] It may be that someone there will not obey the message we send you in this letter. If so, take note of him and have nothing to do with him, so that he will be ashamed. [15] But do not treat him as an enemy; instead, warn him as a brother.

PROVERBS 6:6–11

[6] Lazy people should learn a lesson from the way ants live. [7] They have no leader, chief, or ruler, [8] but they store up their food during the summer, getting ready for winter. [9] How long is the lazy man going to lie around? When is he ever going to get up? [10] "I'll just take a short nap," he says; "I'll fold my hands and rest a while." [11] But while he sleeps, poverty will attack him like an armed robber.

PROVERBS 11:16

[16] A lazy man will never have money,[k] but an aggressive man will get rich.

PROVERBS 13:4

[4] No matter how much a lazy person may want something, he will never get it. A hard worker will get everything he wants.

Keeping Busy

PROVERBS 14:23

[23] Work and you will earn a living; if you sit around talking you will be poor.

PROVERBS 20:13

[13] If you spend your time sleeping, you will be poor. Keep busy and you will have plenty to eat.

PROVERBS 23:21

[21] Drunkards and gluttons will be reduced to poverty. If all you do is eat and sleep, you will soon be wearing rags.

PROVERBS 24:30–34

[30] I walked through the fields and vineyards of a lazy, stupid man. [31] They were full of thorn bushes and overgrown with weeds. The stone wall around them had fallen down. [32] I looked at this, thought about it, and learned a lesson from it: [33] Go ahead and take your nap; go ahead and sleep. Fold your hands and rest awhile, [34] but while you are asleep, poverty will attack you like an armed robber.

PROVERBS 28:19

[19] A hard-working farmer has plenty to eat. People who waste time will always be poor.

OBEDIENCE AND ABUNDANCE

Wisdom and Knowledge

2 CHRONICLES 1:11–12

[11] God replied to Solomon, "You have made the right choice. Instead of asking for wealth or treasure or fame or the death of your enemies or even for long life for yourself, you have asked for wisdom and knowledge so that you can rule my people over whom I have made you king. [12] I will give you wisdom and knowledge. And in addition, I will give you more wealth, treasure, and fame

than any king has ever had before or will ever have again."

The Lord's Blessing

EXODUS 26:12–13

¹² Isaac sowed crops in that land, and that year he harvested a hundred times as much as he had sown, because the LORD blessed him. ¹³ He continued to prosper and became a very rich man.

PSALM 128:1–4

Happy are those who have reverence for the LORD,
   who live by his commands.
² Your work will provide for your needs;
   you will be happy and prosperous.
³ Your wife will be like a fruitful vine in your home,
   and your sons will be like young olive trees around your
      table.
⁴ A man who obeys the LORD
   will surely be blessed like this.

PROVERBS 15:6

⁶ Righteous men keep their wealth, but wicked men lose theirs when hard times come.

ECCLESIASTES 5:19

¹⁹ If God gives a man wealth and property and lets him enjoy them, he should be grateful and enjoy what he has worked for. It is a gift from God.

ABUNDANCE AS DIVINE BLESSING?

A Rich Harvest

LEVITICUS 26:3–5

³ "If you live according to my laws and obey my commands, ⁴ I will send you rain at the right time, so that the land will produce crops and the trees will bear fruit. ⁵ Your crops will be so plentiful that you will still be harvesting grain when it is time to pick grapes, and you will still be picking grapes when it is time to plant grain. You will have all that you want to eat, and you can live in safety in your land.

Obeying God's Commands

LEVITICUS 26:14–16

¹⁴ The LORD said, "If you will not obey my commands, you will be punished. ¹⁵ If you refuse to obey my laws and commands and break the covenant I have made with you, ¹⁶ I will punish you. I will bring disaster on you—incurable diseases and fevers that will make you blind and cause your life to waste away. You will plant your crops, but it will do you no good, because your enemies will conquer you and eat what you have grown.

JOB 31:16–25

¹⁶ I have never refused to help the poor;
   never have I let widows live in despair
¹⁷   or let orphans go hungry while I ate.
¹⁸ All my life I have taken care of them.

¹⁹ When I found someone in need,
   too poor to buy clothes,
²⁰   I would give him clothing made of wool
   that had come from my own flock of sheep.
Then he would praise me with all his heart.

²¹ If I have ever cheated an orphan,
knowing I could win in court,
²² then may my arms be broken;
may they be torn from my shoulders.
²³ Because I fear God's punishment.
I could never do such a thing.

²⁴ I have never trusted in riches
²⁵ or taken pride in my wealth.

Blessed by the Lord

PSALM 37:22–26

²² Those who are blessed by the LORD will possess the land,
but those who are cursed by him will be driven out.

²³ The LORD guides a man in the way he should go
and protects those who please him.
²⁴ If they fall, they will not stay down,
because the LORD will help them up.

²⁵ I am an old man now; I have lived a long time,
but I have never seen a good man abandoned by the
LORD
or his children begging for food.
²⁶ At all times he gives freely and lends to others,
and his children are a blessing.

PSALM 112:1–5, 9
Praise the LORD!

Happy is the person who has reverence for the LORD,
who takes pleasure in obeying his commands.

³ His family will be wealthy and rich,
and he will be prosperous forever.
⁴ Light shines in the darkness for good men,
for those who are merciful, kind, and just.

⁵ Happy is the person who is generous with his loans,
   who runs his business honestly.

⁹ He gives generously to the needy,
   and his kindness never fails.

PROVERBS 8:17–21

¹⁷ I love those who love me;
   whoever looks for me can find me.
¹⁸ I have riches and honor to give,
   prosperity and success.
¹⁹ What you get from me is better than the finest gold,
   better than the purest silver.
²⁰ I walk the way of righteousness;
   I follow the paths of justice,
²¹ giving wealth to those who love me.
   filling their houses with treasures.

PROVERBS 10:22

²² It is the LORD's blessing that makes you wealthy. Hard work can make you no richer.

Be Generous

PROVERBS 11:25–26

²⁵ Be generous, and you will be prosperous. Help others, and you will be helped.
²⁶ People curse a man who hoards grain, waiting for a higher price, but they praise the one who puts it up for sale.

Be Humble

PROVERBS 22:4

⁴ Have reverence for the LORD, be humble, and you will get riches, honor, and a long life.

Give to the Poor

²⁷ Give to the poor and you will never be in need. If you close your eyes to the poor, many people will curse you.

A Capable Wife

¹⁰ How hard it is to find a capable wife! She is worth far more than jewels!

¹³ She keeps herself busy making wool and linen cloth.

¹⁴ She brings home food from out-of-the-way places, as merchant ships do.

¹⁵ She gets up before daylight to prepare food for her family and to tell her servant girls what to do.

¹⁶ She looks at land and buys it, and with money she has earned she plants a vineyard.

¹⁷ She is a hard worker, strong and industrious.

¹⁸ She knows the value of everything she makes, and works late into the night.

¹⁹ She spins her own thread and weaves her own cloth.

²⁰ She is generous to the poor and needy.

²¹ She doesn't worry when it snows, because her family has warm clothing.

²² She makes bedspreads and wears clothes of fine purple linen.

²³ Her husband is well known, one of the leading citizens.

²⁴ She makes clothes and belts, and sells them to merchants.

²⁵ She is strong and respected and not afraid of the future.

V

GOD'S CONCERN FOR JUSTICE

GOD WILLS JUSTICE

Because He Is Lord

DEUTERONOMY 32:4

⁴ "The Lord is your mighty defender, perfect and just in all his ways; your God is faithful and true; he does what is right and fair.

LEVITICUS 19:11–18

¹¹ "Do not steal or cheat or lie. ¹² Do not make a promise in my name if you do not intend to keep it; that brings disgrace on my name. I am the LORD your God.

¹³ "Do not take advantage of anyone or rob him. Do not hold back the wages of someone you have hired, not even for one night. ¹⁴ Do not curse a deaf man or put something in front of a blind man so as to make him stumble over it. Have reverence for me; I am the LORD your God.

¹⁵ "Be honest and just when you make decisions in legal cases; do not show favoritism to the poor or fear the rich. ¹⁶ Do not spread lies about anyone, and when someone is on trial for his life, speak out if your testimony can help him. I am the LORD.

¹⁷ "Do not bear a grudge against anyone, but settle your differences with him, so that you will not commit a sin because of him.ʰ ¹⁸ Do not take revenge on anyone or continue to hate him, but love your neighbor as you love yourself. I am the LORD.

A Case of Injustice

2 SAMUEL 11:1–4, 6, 14–15; 12:1–7

The following spring, at the time of the year when kings usually go to war, David sent out Joab with his officers and the Israelite army; they defeated the Ammonites and besieged the city of Rabbah. But David himself stayed in Jerusalem.

² One day, late in the afternoon, David got up from his nap and went to the palace roof. As he walked around up there, he saw a woman taking a bath in her house. She was very beautiful. ³ So he sent a messenger to find out who she was, and learned that she was Bathsheba, the daughter of Eliam and the wife of Uriah the Hittite. ⁴ David sent messengers to get her; they brought her to him and he made love to her.

⁶ David then sent a message to Joab: "Send me Uriah the Hittite." So Joab sent him to David.

¹⁴ The next morning David wrote a letter to Joab and sent it by Uriah. ¹⁵ He wrote: "Put Uriah in the front line, where the fighting is heaviest, then retreat and let him be killed."

The LORD sent the prophet Nathan to David. Nathan went to him and said, "There were two men who lived in the same town; one was rich and the other poor. ² The rich man had many cattle and sheep, ³ while the poor man had only one lamb, which he had bought. He took care of it, and it grew up in his home with his children. He would feed it some of his own food, let it drink from his cup, and hold it in his lap. The lamb was like a daughter to him. ⁴ One day a visitor arrived at the rich man's home. The rich man didn't want to kill one of his own animals to fix a meal for him; instead he took the poor man's lamb and prepared a meal for his guest."

⁵ David became very angry at the rich man and said, "I swear by the living LORD that the man who did this ought to die! ⁶ For having done such a cruel thing, he must pay back four times as much as he took."

⁷ "You are that man." Nathan said to David.

1 CHRONICLES 18:14

¹⁴ David ruled over all Israel and made sure that his people were always treated fairly and justly.

God Rules the World with Justice

PSALM 9:7–12, 18

7 But the LORD is king forever;
   he has set up his throne for judgment.
8 He rules the world with righteousness;
   he judges the nations with justice.

9 The LORD is a refuge for the oppressed
   a place of safety in times of trouble.
10 Those who know you, LORD, will trust you;
   you do not abandon anyone who comes to you.
11 Sing praise to the LORD, who rules in Zion!
   Tell every nation what he has done!
12 God remembers those who suffer;
   he does not forget their cry,
   and he punishes those who wrong them.

18 The needy will not always be neglected;
   the hope of the poor will not be crushed forever.

PSALM 89:8, 14

8 LORD God Almighty, none is as mighty as you;
   in all things you are faithful, O LORD.

14 Your kingdom is founded on righteousness and justice;
   love and faithfulness are shown in all you do.

Does God Notice Injustice?

PSALM 94:1–15

Lord, you are a God who punishes;
   reveal your anger!
2 You are the judge of all men;
   rise and give the proud what they deserve!
3 How much longer will the wicked be glad?
   How much longer, LORD?

Per Capita Energy Consumption—1973		
country	kilograms per person (coal equivalent)	energy use as multiple of use in Ethiopia
United States	11,960	342
Canada	11,237	321
West Germany	5,792	165
Great Britain	5,778	165
USSR	4,927	141
France	4,389	125
Japan	3,601	103
Italy	2,737	78
Mexico	1,355	39
Brazil	556	16
Philippines	291	8
India	188	5
Pakistan	149	4
Ethiopia	35	1

Source: U.S. Bureau of the Census, Statistical Abstract of the U.S., 1976, pp. 849–50.

⁴ How much longer will criminals be proud
    and boast about their crimes?
⁵ They crush your people, LORD;
    they oppress those who belong to you.
⁶ They kill widows and orphans,
    and murder the strangers who live in our land.
⁷ They say, "The LORD does not see us;
    the God of Israel does not notice."
⁸ My people, how can you be such stupid fools?
    When will you ever learn?

⁹ God made our ears—can't he hear?
   He made our eyes—can't he see?
¹⁰ He is in charge of the nations—won't he punish them?
   He is the teacher of all men—hasn't he any knowledge?
¹¹ The LORD knows what they think;
   he knows how senseless their reasoning is.
¹² LORD, how happy is the person you instruct,
   the one to whom you teach your law!
¹³ You give him rest from days of trouble
   until a pit is dug to trap the wicked.
¹⁴ The LORD will not abandon his people;
   he will not desert those who belong to him.
¹⁵
¹⁵ Justice will again be found in the courts.
   and all righteous people will support it.

Cry Justice

PSALM 96:10–13

¹⁰ Say to all the nations, "The LORD is king!
   The earth is set firmly in place and cannot be moved;
   he will judge the peoples with justice."
¹¹ Be glad, earth and sky!
   Roar, sea, and every creature in you;
   be glad, fields, and everything in you!
¹² The trees in the woods will shout for joy
   when the LORD comes to rule the earth.
¹³ He will rule the peoples of the world
   with justice and fairness.

The King and Justice

PROVERBS 16:11–12

¹¹ The LORD wants weights and measures to be honest and every sale to be fair.

¹² Kings cannot tolerate evil,^b because justice is what makes a government strong.

PROVERBS 28:3

³ A man in authority who oppresses poor people is like a driving rain that destroys the crops.

PROVERBS 29:4

⁴ When the king is concerned with justice, the nation will be strong, but when he is only concerned with money, he will ruin his country.

PROVERBS 29:14

¹⁴ If a king defends the rights of the poor, he will rule for a long time.

PROVERBS 29:26

²⁶ Everybody wants the good will of the ruler, but only from the LORD can you get justice.

Governmental Oppression

ECCLESIASTES 5:8

⁸ Don't be surprised when you see that the government oppresses the poor and denies them justice and their rights. Every official is protected by the one over him, and both are protected by still higher officials.

Hope for Justice

ISAIAH 9:6–7

⁶ A child is born to us!
A son is given to us!
And he will be our ruler.
He will be called, "Wonderful Counselor,"
"Mighty God," "Eternal Father,"
"Prince of Peace."

⁷ His royal power will continue to grow;
his kingdom will always be at peace.

He will rule as King David's successor,
    basing his power on right and justice,
    from now until the end of time.
The Lord Almighty is determined to do all this.

ISAIAH 32:1–3

Some day there will be a king who rules with integrity, and national leaders who govern with justice. [2] Each of them will be like a shelter from the wind and a place to hide from storms. They will be like streams flowing in a desert, like the shadow of a giant rock in a barren land. [3] Their eyes and ears will be open to the needs of the people.

ISAIAH 32:15–17

[15] But once more God will send us his spirit. The wasteland will become fertile, and fields will produce rich crops. [16] Everywhere in the land righteousness and justice will be done. [17] Because everyone will do what is right, there will be peace and security forever.

Justice on Earth

ISAIAH 42:1–7

The Lord says,
    "Here is my servant, whom I strengthen—
the one I have chosen, with whom I am pleased.
I have filled him with my spirit,
    and he will bring justice to every nation.
[2] He will not shout or raise his voice
    or make loud speeches in the streets.
[3] He will not break off a bent reed
    nor put out a flickering lamp.
He will bring lasting justice to all.
[4] He will not lose hope or courage;
    he will establish justice on the earth.
    Distant lands eagerly wait for his teaching."

⁵ God created the heavens and stretched them out;
    he fashioned the earth and all that lives there;
    he gave life and breath to all its people.
And now the LORD God says to his servant,
⁶ "I, the LORD, have called you and given you power
    to see that justice is done on earth.
Through you I will make a covenant with all peoples;
    through you I will bring light to the nations.
⁷ You will open the eyes of the blind
    and set free those who sit in dark prisons.

Justice and Righteousness

JEREMIAH 33:14–15

¹⁴ The LORD said, "The time is coming when I will fulfill the promise that I made to the people of Israel and Judah. ¹⁵At that time I will choose as king a righteous descendant of David. That king will do what is right and just throughout the land.

LAMENTATIONS: 3:34–36

³⁴ The Lord knows when our spirits are crushed in prison. ³⁵ He knows when we are denied the rights he gave us. ³⁶ When justice is perverted in court, he knows.

Let Justice Flow

AMOS 5:21–24

²¹ The LORD says, "I hate your religious festivals; I cannot stand them! ²² When you bring me burnt offerings and grain offerings, I will not accept them; I will not accept the animals you have fattened to bring me as offerings. ²³ Stop your noisy songs; I do not want to listen to your harp. ²⁴ Instead, let justice flow like a stream, and righteousness like a river that never goes dry.

Coming Shalom

MICAH 4:1–4

In days to come
the mountains where the Temple stands
    will be the highest one of all,
    towering above all the hills.
Many nations will come streaming to it,
2   and their people will say,
"Let us go up the hill of the LORD!
    to the Temple of Israel's God.
For he will teach us what he wants us to do;
    we will walk in the paths he has chosen.
For the LORD's teaching comes from Jerusalem;
    from Zion he speaks to his people."

3 He will settle disputes among the nations,
    among the great powers near and far.
They will hammer their swords into plows
    and their spears into pruning knives.
Nations will never again go to war,
    never prepare for battle again.
4 Everyone will live in peace
    among his own vineyards and fig trees,
    and no one will make him afraid.
The LORD Almighty has promised this.

Do What Is Just

MICAH 6:6–8

6 What shall I bring to the LORD, the God of heaven, when I come to worship him? Shall I bring the best calves to burn as offerings to him? 7 Will the LORD be pleased if I bring him thousands of sheep or endless streams of olive oil? Shall I offer him my first-born child to pay for my sins? 8 No, the LORD has told us what is good. What he requires of us is this: to do what is just, to show constant love, and to live in humble fellowship with our God.

¹⁴ The LORD Almighty says, "When your ancestors made me angry, I planned disaster for them and did not change my mind, but carried out my plans. ¹⁵ But now I am planning to bless the people of Jerusalem and Judah. So don't be afraid. ¹⁶ These are the things you should do: Speak the truth to one another. In the courts give real justice—the kind that brings peace. ¹⁷ Do not plan ways of harming one another. Do not give false testimony under oath. I hate lying, injustice, and violence."

Jesus and the Law

MATTHEW 5:17–20

¹⁷ "Do not think that I have come to do away with the Law of Moses and the teachings of the prophets. I have not come to do away with them, but to make their teachings come true. ¹⁸ Remember that as long as heaven and earth last, not the least point nor the smallest detail of the Law will be done away with—not until the end of all things.ᵃ ¹⁹ So then, whoever disobeys even the least important of the commandments and teaches others to do the same, will be least in the Kingdom of heaven. On the other hand, whoever obeys the Law and teaches others to do the same, will be great in the Kingdom of heaven. ²⁰ I tell you, then, that you will be able to enter the Kingdom of heaven only if you are more faithful than the teachers of the Law and the Pharisees in doing what God requires.

MATTHEW 7:12

¹² "Do for others what you want them to do for you: this is the meaning of the Law of Moses and of the teachings of the prophets.

MATTHEW 23:23

²³ "How terrible for you, teachers of the Law and Pharisees! You hypocrites! You give to God one tenth even of the seasoning herbs, such as mint, dill, and cu-

min, but you neglect to obey the really important teachings of the Law, such as justice and mercy and honesty. These you should practice, without neglecting the others.

—LEGAL SYSTEMS—

Judge Fairly

EXODUS 23:6–8
⁶ "Do not deny justice to a poor man when he appears in court. ⁷ Do not make false accusations, and do not put an innocent person to death, for I will condemn anyone who does such an evil thing. ⁸ Do not accept a bribe, for a bribe makes people blind to what is right and ruins the cause of those who are innocent.

DEUTERONOMY 1:16–17
¹⁶ "At that time I instructed them, 'Listen to the disputes that come up among your people. Judge every dispute fairly, whether it concerns only your own people or involves foreigners who live among you. ¹⁷ Show no partiality in your decisions; judge everyone on the same basis, no matter who he is.

The Administration of Justice

DEUTERONOMY 16:18–20
¹⁸ "Appoint judges and other officials in every town that the LORD your God gives you. These men are to judge the people impartially. ¹⁹ They are not to be unjust or show partiality in their judgments; and they are not to accept bribes, for gifts blind the eyes even of wise and honest men, and cause them to give wrong decisions. ²⁰ Always be fair and just, so that you will occupy the land that the LORD your God is giving you and so that you will continue to live there.

PROVERBS 28:21

²¹ Prejudice is wrong. But some judges will do wrong to get even the smallest bribe.

God's Punishment for Unjust Courts

AMOS 5:10–15

¹⁰ You people hate anyone who challenges injustice and speaks the whole truth in court. ¹¹ You have oppressed the poor and robbed them of their grain. And so you will not live in the fine stone houses you build or drink wine from the beautiful vineyards you plant. ¹² I know how terrible your sins are and how many crimes you have committed. You persecute good men, take bribes, and prevent the poor from getting justice in the courts. ¹³ And so, keeping quiet in such evil times is the smart thing to do!

¹⁴ Make it your aim to do what is right, not what is evil, so that you may live. Then the LORD God Almighty really will be with you, as you claim he is. ¹⁵ Hate what is evil, love what is right, and see that justice prevails in the courts. Perhaps the LORD will be merciful to the people of this nation who are still left alive.

—ECONOMIC SYSTEMS—

Do Not Cheat

LEVITICUS 19:35–36

³⁵ "Do not cheat anyone by using false measures of length, weight, or quantity. ³⁶ Use honest scales, honest weights, and honest measures. I am the LORD your God, and I brought you out of Egypt.

DEUTERONOMY 24:10–15

¹⁰ "When you lend a man something, do not go into his house to get the garment he is going to give you as se-

curity; [11] wait outside and let him bring it to you himself.
[12] If he is a poor man, do not keep it overnight; [13] return it
to him each evening, so that he can have it to sleep in.
Then he will be grateful, and the LORD your God will be
pleased with you.

[14] "Do not cheat a poor and needy hired servant,
whether he is a fellow Israelite or a foreigner living in one
of your towns. [15] Each day before sunset pay him for that
day's work; he needs the money and has counted on getting it. If you do not pay him he will cry out against you
to the LORD, and you will be guilty of sin.

DEUTERONOMY 25:13–16

[13-14] "Do not cheat when you use weights and measures. [15] Use true and honest weights and measures, so
that you may live a long time in the land that the LORD
your God is giving you. [16] The LORD hates people who
cheat.

PROVERBS 11:1

The Lord hates people who use dishonest scales. He
is happy with honest weights.

PROVERBS 13:23

[23] Unused fields could yield plenty of food for the
poor, but unjust men keep them from being farmed.[s]

PROVERBS 20:10

[10] The LORD hates people who use dishonest weights
and measures.

Stop Violence and Oppression

EZEKIEL 45:9–10

[9] The Sovereign LORD said, "You have sinned too
long, you rulers of Israel! Stop your violence and oppression. Do what is right and just. You must never again

drive my people off their land. I, the LORD GOD, am telling you this.

¹⁰ "Everyone must use honest weights and measures."

The Lord Is Judge

MALACHI 3:5
⁵ The LORD Almighty says, "I will appear among you to judge, and I will testify at once against those who practice magic, against adulterers, against those who give false testimony, those who cheat employees out of their wages, and those who take advantage of widows, orphans, and foreigners—against all who do not respect me.

INTRODUCTION TO ISAIAH 5:8–16, 22–24

In the eighth century, Israel and Judah enjoyed a time of increased wealth. King Uzziah (783–742) managed a successful foreign policy which brought considerable wealth into Judah. For the rich, this meant increased opportunity. However, for the small landowners it often meant disaster. In verses 8–10 Isaiah describes how the superior economic power of the rich enabled them to appropriate the houses and fields of others. This was especially serious because a family's land was a sacred inheritance in ancient Israel (I Kings 21:1ff).

Isaiah also provides a sad description of the nobility trapped in drunkenness. They mix their drinks (v. 22) to make them more potent (probably a beer made with mixtures of corn, and with certain herbs added), and in the atmosphere of their feasts they disobey Yahweh and oppress the poor. Yahweh abhors both their economic oppression of the poor and their drunken revelry which the oppression supports.

For further study: *in addition to BB, IB, NBC, and NCC, see also G. B. Gray,* A Critical and Exegetical Commentary on the Book of Isaiah, I-XXVII *(ICC, New*

York: *Charles Scribner's Sons, 1912); Otto Kaiser, Isaiah 1–12 (Philadelphia: The Westminster Press, 1972).*

Drunkenness and Economic Oppression

ISAIAH 5:8–13, 15–16, 22–24

⁸ You are doomed! You buy more houses and fields to add to those you already have. Soon there will be no place for anyone else to live, and you alone will live in the land. ⁹ I have heard the LORD Almighty say, "All these big, fine houses will be empty ruins. ¹⁰ The grapevines growing on five acres of land will yield only five gallons of wine. Ten bushels of seed will produce only one bushel of grain."

¹¹ You are doomed! You get up early in the morning to start drinking, and you spend long evenings getting drunk. ¹² At your feasts you have harps and tambourines and flutes—and wine. But you don't understand what the LORD is doing, ¹³ and so you will be carried away as prisoners.

¹⁵ Everyone will be disgraced, and all who are proud will be humbled. ¹⁶ But the LORD Almighty shows his greatness by doing what is right and he reveals his holiness by judging his people.

²² You are doomed! Heroes of the wine bottle! Brave and fearless when it comes to mixing drinks! ²³ But for just a bribe you let guilty men go free, and you keep the innocent from getting justice. ²⁴ So now, just as straw and dry grass shrivel and burn in the fire, your roots will rot and your blossoms will dry up and blow away, because you have rejected what the LORD Almighty, Israel's holy God, has taught us.

A Just Person

EZEKIEL 18:5–9

⁵ "Suppose there is a truly good man, righteous and honest. ⁶ He doesn't worship the idols of the Israelites or

170

eat the sacrifices offered at forbidden shrines. He doesn't seduce another man's wife or have intercourse with a woman during her period. [7] He doesn't cheat or rob anyone. He returns what a borrower gives him as security; he feeds the hungry and gives clothing to the naked. [8] He doesn't lend money for profit. He refuses to do evil and gives an honest decision in any dispute. [9] Such a man obeys my commands and carefully keeps my laws. He is righteous, and he will live," says the Sovereign LORD.

Things That Disgust God

EZEKIEL 22:1–3, 6–12, 15–16

The LORD spoke to me. [2] "Mortal man," he said, "are you ready to judge the city that is full of murderers? Make clear to her all the disgusting things she has done. [3] Tell the city what I, the Sovereign LORD, am saying: Because you have murdered so many of your own people and have defiled yourself by worshiping your time is coming.

[6] "All Israel's leaders trust in their own strength and commit murder. [7] No one in the city honors his parents. You cheat foreigners and take advantage of widows and orphans. [8] You have no respect for the holy places, and you don't keep the Sabbath. [9] Some of your people tell lies about others in order to have them put to death. Some of them eat sacrifices offered to idols. Some are always satisfying their lusts. [10] Some of them sleep with their father's wife. Some force women to have intercourse with them during their period. [11] Some commit adultery, and others seduce their daughters-in-law or their half sisters. [12] Some of your people murder for pay. Some charge interest on the loans they make to their fellow Israelites and get rich by taking advantage of them. They have forgotten me." The Sovereign LORD has spoken.

[15] "I will scatter your people to every country and nation and will put an end to your evil actions. [16] And so

the other nations will dishonor you, but you will know
that I am the LORD."

AMOS 2:6–8

⁶ The LORD says, "The people of Israel have sinned
again and again, and for this I will certainly punish them.
They sell into slavery honest men who cannot pay their
debts, poor men who cannot repay even the price of a
pair of sandals. ⁷ They trampleᵇ down the weak and helpless and push the poor out of the way. A man and his father have intercourse with the same slave girl, and so
profane my holy name. ⁸ At every place of worship men
sleep on clothing that they have taken from the poor as
security for debts. In the temple of their God they drink
wine which they have taken from those who owe them
money.

LEGALIZED OPPRESSION

Unjust Laws

INTRODUCTION TO ISAIAH 10:1–4

*As was noted in Lesson III, Isaiah began his ministry
during a time of prosperity and security in the kingdoms of
Israel and Judah. But not everyone enjoyed this prosperity.
In the previous passage Isaiah severely condemns the oppression of the poor by the ungodly nobility. Many com-
mentators consider 10:1–4, often referred to as "the
seventh woe," to be connected to 5:8–24.*

*In this passage, Isaiah attacks those officials who cre-
ate laws favoring their own interests and the interests of
the rich. Specifically, these laws made it possible for the
rich to acquire the land of the poor, and were thus no
doubt the groundwork for the abuses Isaiah cites in 5:8ff.
Again, land was understood in ancient Israel to be a sa-*

cred inheritance. In this light Isaiah angrily points out that the legal structures simply do not reflect the will of Yahweh. They offer no protection to the poor.

For further study: *in addition to BB, IB, NBC, and NCC, see also G. B. Gray,* A Critical and Exegetical Commentary of the Book of Isaiah, I-XXVII *(ICC, New York: Charles Scribner's Sons, 1912; Otto Kaiser,* Isaiah 1–12 *(Philadelphia: The Westminster Press, 1972).*

ISAIAH 10:1–4

You are doomed! You make unjust laws that oppress my people. ² That is how you keep the poor from having their rights and from getting justice. That is how you take the property that belongs to widows and orphans. ³ What will you do when God punishes you? What will you do when he brings disaster on you from a distant country? Where will you run to find help? Where will you hide your wealth? ⁴ You will be killed in battle or dragged off as prisoners. Yet even so the LORD's anger will not be ended; his hand will still be stretched out to punish.

PSALM 94:20–23

20 You have nothing to do with corrupt judges,
    who make injustice legal,
21 who plot against good men
    and sentence the innocent to death.
22 But the LORD defends me;
    my God protects me.
23 He will punish them for their wickedness
    and destroy them for their sins;
    the LORD our God will destroy them.

GOD'S RESPONSE TO STRUCTURAL SIN

The Fate of Jerusalem

INTRODUCTION TO MICAH 3:1-4, 9-12
  Micah prophesied in the same historical and social context as did Isaiah (see Lesson III) in the latter third of the eighth century. Micah's place in the history of the prophets is significant, for he may have been the first to prophesy the total destruction of Jerusalem (a city thought to be Yahweh's holy and inviolate dwelling place). Later when Jeremiah was threatened with death for this same radical prediction, a section of this prophecy of Micah was cited in his defense (Jer. 26:17ff).

  Micah was horrified at the complete reversal of proper standards of justice. He presents with vivid imagery a picture of vicious and systematic violence inflicted on the helpless by the powerful (vv. 2-3) who turn "right into wrong" (v. 9, literally: "twist all that is straight").

  Even the priests and prophets were caught up in this exploitative greed. According to Israelite judicial practice, the most difficult cases were often brought before the priests who discerned the judgment of Yahweh. In order to remain in good standing with the wealthy and powerful, however, the priests consistently manipulated the law in their favor. For a fee, the members of the prophetic guilds could also be swayed (vv. 5, 11). Micah harshly insists that just as the leaders of Judah have been deaf to the just cries of the poor, Yahweh will ignore their cry on the day of destruction (v. 4).

  For further study: *in addition to BB, IB, ICC, NBC, and NCC, see also James Luther Mays,* Micah *(Philadelphia: The Westminster Press, 1976).*

174

Listen your rulers of Israel! You are supposed to be concerned about justice, ² yet you hate what is good and love what is evil. You skin my people alive and tear the flesh off their bones. ³ You eat my people up. You strip off their skin, break their bones, and chop them up like meat for the pot. ⁴ The time is coming when you will cry out to the LORD, but he will not answer you. He will not listen to your prayers, for you have done evil.

⁹ Listen to me, you rulers of Israel, you that hate justice and turn right into wrong. ¹⁰ You are building God's city, Jerusalem, on a foundation of murder and injustice. ¹¹ The city's rulers govern for bribes, the priests interpret the Law for pay, the prophets give their revelations for money—and they all claim that the LORD is with them. "No harm will come to us," they say. "The LORD is with us."

¹² And so, because of you, Zion will be plowed like a field, Jerusalem will become a pile of ruins, and the Temple hill will become a forest.

Ahab's Punishment

1 KINGS 21:1–19

Near King Ahab's palace in Jezreel there was a vineyard owned by a man named Naboth. ² One day Ahab said to Naboth, "Let me have your vineyard; it is close to my palace, and I want to use the land for a vegetable garden. I will give you a better vineyard for it or, if you prefer, I will pay you a fair price."

³ "I inherited this vineyard from my ancestors," Naboth replied. "The LORD forbid that I should let you have it!"

⁴ Ahab went home, depressed and angry over what Naboth had said to him. He lay down on his bed, facing the wall, and would not eat. ⁵ His wife Jezebel went to him and asked, "Why are you so depressed? Why won't you eat?"

⁶ He answered, "Because of what Naboth said to me. I offered to buy his vineyard or, if he preferred, to give him another one for it, but he told me that I couldn't have it!"

⁷ "Well, are you the king or aren't you?" Jezebel replied. "Get out of bed, cheer up, and eat. I will get you Naboth's vineyard!"

⁸ Then she wrote some letters, signed Ahab's name to them, sealed them with his seal, and sent them to the officials and leading citizens of Jezreel. ⁹ The letters said: "Proclaim a day of fasting, call the people together, and give Naboth the place of honor. ¹⁰ Get a couple of scoundrels to accuse him to his face of cursing God and the king. Then take him out of the city and stone him to death."

¹¹ The officials and leading citizens of Jezreel did what Jezebel had commanded. ¹² They proclaimed a day of fasting, called the people together, and gave Naboth the place of honor. ¹³ The two scoundrels publicly accused him of cursing God and the king, and so he was taken outside the city and stoned to death. ¹⁴ The message was sent to Jezebel: "Naboth has been put to death."

¹⁵ As soon as Jezebel received the message, she said to Ahab, "Naboth is dead. Now go and take possession of the vineyard which he refused to sell to you." ¹⁶ At once Ahab went to the vineyard to take possession of it.

¹⁷ Then the LORD said to Elijah, the prophet from Tishbe, ¹⁸ "Go to King Ahab of Samaria. You will find him in Naboth's vineyard, about to take possession of it. ¹⁹ Tell him that I, the LORD, say to him, 'After murdering the man, are you taking over his property as well?' Tell him that this is what I say: 'In the very place that the dogs licked up Naboth's blood they will lick up your blood!' "

PROVERBS 20:28

²⁸ A king will remain in power as long as his rule is honest, just, and fair.

God's Revenge

²¹ The city that once was faithful is behaving like a whore! At one time it was filled with righteous men, but now only murderers remain. ²² Jerusalem, you were once like silver, but now you are worthless; you were like good wine, but now you are only water. ²³ Your leaders are rebels and friends of thieves; they are always accepting gifts and bribes. They never defend orphans in court or listen when widows present their case.

²⁴ So now, listen to what the LORD Almighty, Israel's powerful God, is saying: "I will take revenge on you, my enemies, and you will cause me no more trouble. ²⁵ I will take action against you. I will purify you the way metal is refined, and will remove all your impurity. ²⁶ I will give you rulers and advisers like those you had long ago. Then Jerusalem will be called the righteous, faithful city."

Change Your Ways

JEREMIAH 7:1–15

¹⁻³ The LORD sent me to the gate of the Temple where the people of Judah went in to worship. He told me to stand there and announce what the LORD Almighty, the God of Israel, had to say to them: "Change the way you are living and the things you are doing, and I will let you go on living here. ⁴ Stop believing those deceitful words, 'We are safe! This is the LORD's Temple, this is the LORD's Temple!'

⁵ "Change the way you are living and stop doing the things you are doing. Be fair in your treatment of one another. ⁶ Stop taking advantage of aliens, orphans, and widows. Stop killing innocent people in this land. Stop worshiping other gods, for that will destroy you. ⁷ If you change, I will let you go on living here in the land which I gave your ancestors as a permanent possession.

8 "Look, you put your trust in deceitful words. 9 You steal, murder, commit adultery, tell lies under oath, offer sacrifices to Baal, and worship gods that you had not known before. 10 You do these things I hate, and then you come and stand in my presence, in my own Temple, and say, 'We are safe!' 11 Do you think that my Temple is a hiding place for robbers? I have seen what you are doing. 12 Go to Shiloh,ᵉ the first place where I chose to be worshiped, and see what I did to it because of the sins of my people Israel. 13 You have committed all these sins, and even though I spoke to you over and over again, you refused to listen. You would not answer when I called you. 14 And so, what I did to Shiloh I will do to this Temple of mine, in which you trust. Here in this place that I gave to your ancestors and you, I will do the same thing that I did to Shiloh. 15 I will drive you out of my sight as I drove out your relatives, the people of Israel. I, the LORD, have spoken."

Rejection of God's Chosen Nation

JEREMIAH 12:1-2, 5, 7

LORD, if I argued my case with you,
  you would prove to be right.
Yet I must question you about matters of justice.
Why are wicked men so prosperous?
  Why do dishonest men succeed?
2 You plant them, and they take root;
  they grow and bear fruit.
They always speak well of you,
  yet they do not really care about you.

5 The LORD said,
"Jeremiah, if you get tired racing against men,
  how can you race against horses?

[7] The LORD says,
   "I have abandoned Israel;
      I have rejected my chosen nation.
   I have given the people I love
      into the power of their enemies.

The Terrible Drought

JEREMIAH 14:1–6, 11–16

[1] The LORD said to me concerning the drought,
[2] "Judah is in mourning;
      its cities are dying,
   its people lie on the ground in sorrow,
      and Jerusalem cries out for help.
[3] The rich people send their servants for water;
      they go to the cisterns,
      but find no water;
      they come back with their jars empty.
   Discouraged and confused,
      they hide their faces.
[4] Because there is no rain
      and the ground is dried up.
   the farmers are sick at heart;
      they hide their faces.
[5] In the field the mother deer
      abandons her newborn fawn
      because there is no grass.
[6] The wild donkeys stand on the hilltops
      and pant for breath like jackals;
   their eyesight fails them
      because they have no food.

[11] The LORD said to me, "Do not ask me to help these people. [12] Even if they fast, I will not listen to their cry for help; and even if they offer me burnt offerings and grain offerings, I will not be pleased with them. Instead, I will kill them in war and by starvation and disease."

¹³ Then I said, "Sovereign LORD, you know that the prophets are telling the people that there will be no war or starvation, because you have promised, they say, that there will be only peace in our land."

¹⁴ But the LORD replied, "The prophets are telling lies in my name; I did not send them, nor did I give them any orders or speak one word to them. The visions they talk about have not come from me; their predictions are worthless things that they have imagined. ¹⁵ I, the LORD, tell you what I am going to do to those prophets whom I did not send but who speak in my name and say war and starvation will not strike this land—I will kill them in war and by starvation. ¹⁶ The people to whom they have said these things will be killed in the same way. Their bodies will be thrown out into the streets of Jerusalem, and there will be no one to bury them. This will happen to all of them—including their wives, their sons, and their daughters. I will make them pay for their wickedness."

Building One's House by Injustice

INTRODUCTION TO JEREMIAH 22:13–19

Jeremiah's ministry during the later seventh and early sixth centuries covered a most turbulent and critical era for the people of Judah. A few years before Jeremiah uttered this prophecy, the late King Josiah, whom Jeremiah praises in verses 15–16 as a king who encouraged fair treatment of the poor, had managed to free Judah from Assyrian control. But after his death, Josiah was replaced by his son Jehoahaz, who after only a few months was led away captive into Egypt. The Egyptian Pharaoh Neco replaced him with Jehoiakim, Josiah's second son.

Jehoiakim was a horribly corrupt and selfish king. Though the people were already badly crippled economically, Jehoiakim wanted an extravagant palace for himself. This structure was built by forced labor of citizens who never received the wages they deserved (v. 13). The

180

luxurious edifice served as a false mask of kingship (2:15) for a scoundrel who could hardly be described as a king, at least not by the standards of Yahweh (v. 16).

The dreadful nature of the fate Jeremiah foresees for Jehoiakim can hardly be grasped by the modern reader. To be dragged dead from the city like a beast of burden and left uninterred outside the gates (v. 19) would have been an almost unspeakable horror in the mind of the ancient Semite. Indeed, modern scholars think it likely that Jehoiakim was in fact assassinated in dishonor at the time of Babylonian advancement in 598–587.

For further study: *in addition to BB, IB, NBC, and NCC, see also John Bright,* Jeremiah *("The Anchor Bible," New York: Doubleday & Co., Inc., 1965); R. K. Harrison,* Jeremiah and Lamentations *(TOT, Downers Grove: Inter-Varsity Press, 1973).*

JEREMIAH 22:13–19

¹³ Doomed is the man who builds his house by injustice
    and enlarges it by dishonesty;
who makes his countrymen work for nothing
    and does not pay their wages.
¹⁴ Doomed is the man who says,
    "I will build myself a mansion
    with spacious rooms upstairs."
So he puts windows in his house,
    panels it with cedar,
    and paints it red.
¹⁵ Does it make you a better king
    if you build houses of cedar,
    finer than those of others?
Your father enjoyed a full life.
    He was always just and fair,
    and he prospered in everything he did.
¹⁶ He gave the poor a fair trial,
    and all went well with him.
That is what it means to know the LORD.

¹⁷ But you can only see your selfish interests;
  you kill the innocent
  and violently oppress your people.
The LORD has spoken.
¹⁸ So then, the LORD says about Josiah's son Jehoiakim, king
    of Judah,
  "No one will mourn his death or say,
    'How terrible, my friend, how terrible!'
  No one will weep for him or cry,
    'My lord! My king!'
¹⁹ With the funeral honors of a donkey,
  he will be dragged away
  and thrown outside Jerusalem's gates."

Destruction of Jerusalem

LAMENTATIONS 1:1, 11

  How lonely lies Jerusalem, once so full of people!
    Once honored by the world, she is now like a widow;
    The noblest of cities has fallen into slavery.

¹¹ Her people groan as they look for something to eat;
    They exchange their treasures for food to keep
      themselves alive.
    "Look at me, LORD," the city cries; "see me in my
      misery."

LAMENTATIONS 2:11–12, 19–20

¹¹ My eyes are worn out with weeping; my soul is in anguish.
    I am exhausted with grief at the destruction of my
      people.
    Children and babies are fainting in the streets of the
      city.

¹² Hungry and thirsty, they cry to their mothers;
    They fall in the streets as though they were wounded,
    And slowly die in their mothers' arms.

¹⁹ All through the night get up again and again to cry out to
      the Lord;
    Pour out your heart and beg him for mercy on your
      children—
    Children starving to death on every street corner!

²⁰ Look, O LORD! Look at those you are making suffer!
    Women are eating the bodies of the children they loved!
    Priests and prophets are being killed in the Temple
      itself!

LAMENTATIONS 4:9–10
⁹ Those who died in the war were better off than those who
      died later,
    who starved slowly to death, with no food to keep them
      alive.
¹⁰ The disaster that came to my people brought horror;
    loving mothers boiled their own children for food.

Nebuchadnezzar's Punishment

DANIEL 4:24–28
²⁴ "This, then, is what it means, Your Majesty, and
this is what the Supreme God has declared will happen to
you. ²⁵ You will be driven away from human society and
will live with wild animals. For seven years you will eat
grass like an ox and sleep in the open air, where the dew
will fall on you. Then you will admit that the Supreme
God controls all human kingdoms and that he can give
them to anyone he chooses. ²⁶ The angels ordered the
stump to be left in the ground. This means that you will
become king again when you acknowledge that God rules
all the world. ²⁷ So then, Your Majesty, follow my advice.
Stop sinning, do what is right, and be merciful to the
poor.^f Then you will continue to be prosperous."
²⁸ All this did happen to King Nebuchadnezzar.

Drought and Famine

AMOS 4:6–9

⁶ "I was the one who brought famine to all your cities, yet you did not come back to me. ⁷ I kept it from raining when your crops needed it most. I sent rain on one city, but not on another. Rain fell on one field, but another field dried up. ⁸ Weak with thirst, the people of several cities went to a city where they hoped to find water, but there was not enough to drink. Still you did not come back to me.

⁹ "I sent a scorching wind to dry up your crops. The locusts ate up all your gardens and vineyards, your fig trees and olive trees. Still you did not come back to me.

Twisting Justice

AMOS 5:6–9

⁶ Go to the LORD, and you will live. If you do not go, he will sweep down like fire on the people of Israel. The fire will burn up the people of Bethel, and no one will be able to put it out. ⁷ You are doomed, you that twist justice and cheat people out of their rights!

⁸ The LORD made the stars,
  the Pleiades and Orion.
He turns darkness into daylight
  and day into night.
He calls for the waters of the sea
  and pours them out on the earth.
His name is the LORD.
⁹ He brings destruction on the mighty and their strongholds.

Israel Warned of Exile

AMOS 6:4–7

⁴ How terrible it will be for you that stretch out on your luxurious couches, feasting on veal and lamb! ⁵ You

184

like to compose songs, as David did, and play them on harps. ⁶ You drink wine by the bowlful and use the finest perfumes, but you do not mourn over the ruin of Israel. ⁷ So you will be the first to go into exile.'"

¹⁰ Amaziah, the priest of Bethel, then sent a report to King Jeroboam of Israel: "Amos is plotting against you among the people. His speeches will destroy the country. ¹¹ This is what he says: 'Jeroboam will die in battle, and the people of Israel will be taken away from their land into exile.'"

¹² Amaziah then said to Amos, "That's enough, prophet! Go on back to Judah and do your preaching there. Let *them* pay for it. ¹³ Don't prophesy here at Bethel any more. This is the king's place of worship, the national temple."

¹⁴ Amos answered, "I am not the kind of prophet who prophesies for pay. I am a herdsman, and I take care of fig trees. ¹⁵ But the LORD took me from my work as a shepherd and ordered me to go and prophesy to his people Israel. ¹⁶ So now listen to what the LORD says. You tell me to stop prophesying, to stop raving against the people of Israel. ¹⁷ And so, Amaziah, the LORD says to you, 'Your wife will become a prostitute in the city, and your children will be killed in war. Your land will be divided up and given to others, and you yourself will die in a heathen country. And the people of Israel will certainly be taken away from their own land into exile.'"

A Different Kind of Famine

¹¹ "The time is coming when I will send famine on the land. People will be hungry, but not for bread; they will be thirsty, but not for water. They will hunger and thirst for a message from the LORD. I, the Sovereign LORD, have spoken. ¹² People will wander from the Dead

Sea to the Mediterranean and then on around from the north to the east. They will look everywhere for a message from the LORD, but they will not find it.

Wealth and Glamor Gone

REVELATION 18:1–3, 9–15, 24

After this I saw another angel coming down out of heaven. He had great authority, and his splendor brightened the whole earth. ² He cried out in a loud voice: "She has fallen! Great Babylon has fallen! She is now haunted by demons and unclean spirits; all kinds of filthy and hateful birds live in her. ³ For all the nations have drunk her wine—the strong wine of her immortal lust. The kings of the earth practiced sexual immorality with her, and the businessmen of the world grew rich from her unrestrained lust."

⁹ The kings of the earth who took part in her immorality and lust will cry and weep over the city when they see the smoke from the flames that consume her. ¹⁰ They stand a long way off, because they are afraid of sharing in her suffering. They say, "How terrible! How awful! This great and mighty city Babylon! In just one hour you have been punished!"

¹¹ The businessmen of the earth also cry and mourn for her, because no one buys their goods any longer; ¹² no one buys their gold, silver, precious stones, and pearls; their goods of linen, purple cloth, silk, and scarlet cloth; all kinds of rare woods and all kinds of objects made of ivory and of expensive wood, of bronze, iron, and marble; ¹³ and cinnamon, spice, incense, myrrh, and frankincense; wine and oil, flour and wheat, cattle and sheep, horses and carriages, slaves, and even human lives. ¹⁴ The businessmen say to her, "All the good things you longed to own have disappeared, and all your wealth and glamor are gone, and you will never find them again!" ¹⁵ The businessmen, who became rich from doing business in

that city, will stand a long way off, because they are afraid of sharing in her suffering.

²⁴ Babylon was punished because the blood of prophets and of God's people was found in the city; yes, the blood of all those who have been killed on earth.

VI

AN INVITATION TO RESPONSIBLE STEWARDSHIP AND COSTLY DISCIPLESHIP

The Romans learned the brutal practice of crucifixion from the Carthaginians and used it to insure that executions would be both painful and humiliating (they forced the victim to carry his own crossbeam to the place of crucifixion). Jesus however refers to the cross not as a symbol of despair, but rather as a symbol of profound victory—victory through ultimate self-denial.

It is in this context that this puzzling passage is to be understood. Jesus knows that to follow him faithfully is to threaten the customs and structures of the world, and therefore to court persecution. His disciples must understand that following him will often involve costly confrontation. And so, he warns that allegiance to him must not be conditional. Jesus demands that we love him even more than our family relations.

For further study: *in addition to BB, IB, ICC, NBC, and NCC, see also Eduard Schweitzer,* The Good News According to Matthew, *trans. David E. Green (Atlanta: The John Knox Press, 1975); R. V. G. Tasker,* The Gospel According to St. Matthew *(TNT, Grand Rapids: Eerdmans Publishing Co., 1961).*

On Being a Disciple

MATTHEW **10:37–39**

[37] "Whoever loves his father or mother more than me is not fit to be my disciple; whoever loves his son or daughter more than me is not fit to be my disciple. [38] Whoever does not take up his cross and follow in my steps is not fit to be my disciple. [39] Whoever tries to gain his own life will lose it; but whoever loses his life for my sake will gain it.

GENESIS 1:26–31

²⁶ Then God said, "And now we will make human beings; they will be like us and resemble us. They will have power over the fish, the birds, and all animals, domestic and wild,ᵈ large and small." ²⁷ So God created human beings, making them to be like himself. He created them male and female, ²⁸ blessed them, and said, "Have many children, so that your descendants will live all over the earth and bring it under their control. I am putting you in charge of the fish, the birds, and all the wild animals. ²⁹ I have provided all kinds of grain and all kinds of fruit for you to eat; ³⁰ but for all the wild animals and for all the birds I have provided grass and leafy plants for food"—and it was done. ³¹ God looked at everything he had made, and he was very pleased. Evening passed and morning came—that was the sixth day.

INTRODUCTION TO PSALM 8

Psalm 8 has been called, along with Psalms 19 (vv. 1–6), 29, and 104, one of the cosmic hymns. It affirms the kingship of Yahweh over all creation ("he is a great king, ruling over all the world"—Ps. 47:2). Psalm 8 was probably intended for the use of the whole congregation in public worship (its general, non-specific nature tends to indicate this).

For further study: *in addition to BB, IB, NBC, and NCC, see also C. A. Briggs, Psalms, Vol. I (ICC; Edinburgh: T & T Clark, 1914); Derek Kidner, Psalms 1–72 (TOT, Downers Grove: Inter-Varsity Press, 1973); Leopold Sabourin, S.J., The Psalms: Their Origin and Meaning (New York: Alba House, 1969); Arthur Weiser, The Psalms, trans. H. Hartwell (London: SCM Press, Ltd., 1962).*

Placed Over All Creation

PSALM 8:1–9

    O LORD, our Lord,
        your greatness is seen in all the world!
    Your praise reaches up to the heavens;
²   it is sung by children and babies.
    You are safe and secure from all your enemies;
        you stop anyone who opposes you.

³ When I look at the sky, which you have made,
        at the moon and the stars, which you set in their
            places—
⁴ what is man, that you think of him;
        mere man, that you care for him?
⁵ Yet you made him inferior only to yourself;
        you crowned him with glory and honor.
⁶ You appointed him ruler over everything you made;
        you placed him over all creation:
⁷   sheep and cattle, and the wild animals too;
⁸   the birds and the fish
    and the creatures in the seas.

⁹ O LORD, our Lord,
        your greatness is seen in all the world!

The Parable of the Three Servants

MATTHEW 25:14–30

¹⁴ "At that time the Kingdom of heaven will be like this. Once there was a man who was about to leave home on a trip; he called his servants and put them in charge of his property. ¹⁵ He gave to each one according to his ability: to one he gave five thousand silver coins, to another he gave two thousand, and to another he gave one thousand. Then he left on his trip. ¹⁶ The servant who had received five thousand coins went at once and invested his money and earned another five thousand. ¹⁷ In the same

way the servant who had received two thousand coins earned another two thousand. [18] But the servant who had received one thousand coins went off, dug a hole in the ground, and hid his master's money.

[19] "After a long time the master of those servants came back and settled accounts with them. [20] The servant who had received five thousand coins came in and handed over the other five thousand. 'You gave me five thousand coins, sir,' he said. 'Look! Here are another five thousand that I have earned.' [21] 'Well done, you good and faithful servant!' said his master. 'You have been faithful in managing small amounts, so I will put you in charge of large amounts. Come on in and share my happiness!' [22] Then the servant who had been given two thousand coins came in and said, 'You gave me two thousand coins, sir. Look! Here are another two thousand that I have earned.' [23] 'Well done, you good and faithful servant!' said his master. 'You have been faithful in managing small amounts, so I will put in charge of large amounts. Come on in and share my happiness!' [24] Then the servant who had received one thousand coins came and said, 'Sir, I know you are a hard man; you reap harvests where you did not plant, and you gather crops where you did not scatter seed. [25] I was afraid, so I went off and hid your money in the ground. Look! Here is what belongs to you.' [26] 'You bad and lazy servant!' his master said. 'You knew, did you, that I reap harvests where I did not plant, and gather crops where I did not scatter seed? [27] Well, then, you should have deposited my money in the bank, and I would have received it all back with interest when I returned. [28] Now, take the money away from him and give it to the one who has ten thousand coins. [29] For to every person who has something, even more will be given, and he will have more than enough; but the person who has nothing, even the little that he has will be taken away from him. [30] As for this useless servant—throw him outside in the darkness; there he will cry and gnash his teeth.'

The Widow's Offering

MARK 12:41–44

⁴¹ As Jesus sat near the temple treasury, he watched the people as they dropped in their money. Many rich men dropped in a lot of money; ⁴² then a poor widow came along and dropped in two little copper coins, worth about a penny. ⁴³ He called his disciples together and said to them, "I tell you that this poor widow put more in the offering box than all the others. ⁴⁴ For the others put in what they had to spare of their riches; but she, poor as she is, put in all she had—she gave all she had to live on."

The Would-Be Followers of Jesus

LUKE 9:57–62

⁵⁷ As they went on their way, a man said to Jesus, "I will follow you wherever you go."

⁵⁸ Jesus said to him, "Foxes have holes, and birds have nests, but the Son of Man has no place to lie down and rest."

⁵⁹ He said to another man, "Follow me."

But that man said, "Sir, first let me go back and bury my father."

⁶⁰ Jesus answered, "Let the dead bury their own dead. You go and proclaim the Kingdom of God."

⁶¹ Another man said, "I will follow you, sir; but first let me go and say good-bye to my family."

⁶² Jesus said to him, "Anyone who starts to plow and then keeps looking back is of no use for the Kingdom of God."

The Cost of Being a Disciple

LUKE 14:25–33

²⁵ Once when large crowds of people were going along with Jesus, he turned and said to them, ²⁶ "Whoev-

er comes to me cannot be my disciple unless he loves me more than he loves his father and his mother, his wife and his children, his brothers and his sisters, and himself as well. ²⁷ Whoever does not carry his own cross and come after me cannot be my disciple. ²⁸ If one of you is planning to build a tower, he sits down first and figures out what it will cost, to see if he has enough money to finish the job. ²⁹ If he doesn't, he will not be able to finish the tower after laying the foundation; and all who see what happened will make fun of him. ³⁰ 'This man began to build but can't finish the job!' they will say. ³¹ If a king goes out with ten thousand men to fight another king who comes against him with twenty thousand men, he will sit down first and decide if he is strong enough to face that other kind. ³² If he isn't, he will send messengers to meet the other king to ask for terms of peace while he is still a long way off. ³³ In the same way," concluded Jesus, "none of you can be my disciple unless he gives up everything he has.

Christian Freedom

ROMANS 14:1–12

Welcome the person who is weak in faith, but do not argue with him about his personal opinions. ² One person's faith allows him to eat anything, but the person who is weak in the faith eats only vegetables. ³ The person who will eat anything is not to despise the one who doesn't; while the one who eats only vegetables is not to pass judgment on the one who will eat anything; for God has accepted him. ⁴ Who are you to judge the servant of someone else? It is his own master who will decide whether he succeeds or fails. And he will succeed, because the Lord is able to make him succeed.

⁵ One person thinks that a certain day is more important than other days, while someone else thinks that all days are the same. Each one should firmly make up his own mind. ⁶ Whoever thinks highly of a certain day

does so in honor of the Lord; whoever will eat anything does so in honor of the Lord, because he gives thanks to God for the food. Whoever refuses to eat certain things does so in honor of the Lord, and he gives thanks to God. [7] None of us lives for himself only, none of us dies for himself only. [8] If we live, it is for the Lord that we live, and if we die, it is for the Lord that we die. So whether we live or die, we belong to the Lord. [9] For Christ died and rose to life in order to be the Lord of the living and of the dead. [10] You then, who eat only vegetables—why do you pass judgment on your brother? And you who eat anything—why do you despise your brother? All of us will stand before God to be judged by him. [11] For the scripture says,

> "As surely as I am the living God, says the Lord,
> everyone will kneel before me,
> and everyone will confess that I am God."

[12] Every one of us, then, will have to give an account of
himself to God.

The Preeminence of Love

1 CORINTHIANS 13:1–3

I may be able to speak the languages of men and even of angels, but if I have no love, my speech is no more than a noisy gong or a clanging bell. [2] I may have the gift of inspired preaching; I may have all knowledge and understand all secrets; I may have all the faith needed to move mountains—but if I have no love, I am nothing. [3] I may give away everything I have, and even give up my body to be burned[n]—but if I have no love, this does me no good.

Practice the Word

JAMES 1:22-24

²² Do not deceive yourselves by just listening to his word; instead, put it into practice. ²³ Whoever listens to the word but does not put it into practice is like a man who looks in a mirror and sees himself as he is. ²⁴ He takes a good look at himself and then goes away and at once forgets what he looks like.

JAMES 4:17

¹⁷ So then, the person who does not do the good he knows he should do is guilty of sin.

True Happiness

MATTHEW 5:1-12

Jesus saw the crowds and went up a hill, where he sat down. His disciples gathered around him, ² and he began to teach them:

³ "Happy are those who know they are spiritually poor;
    the Kingdom of heaven belongs to them!
⁴ "Happy are those who mourn;
    God will comfort them!
⁵ "Happy are those who are humble·
    they will receive what God has promised!
⁶ "Happy are those whose greatest desire is to do what God
        requires;
    God will satisfy them fully!
⁷ "Happy are those who are merciful to others;
    God will be merciful to them!
⁸ "Happy are the pure in heart;
    they will see God!
⁹ "Happy are those who work for peace;
    God will call them his children!

[10] "Happy are those who are persecuted because they do what God requires;
the Kingdom of heaven belongs to them!

[11] "Happy are you when people insult you and persecute you and tell all kinds of evil lies against you because you are my followers. [12] Be happy and glad, for a great reward is kept for you in heaven. This is how the prophets who lived before you were persecuted.

STUDY QUESTIONS

The study questions in the following lessons are all tough, weighty ones. They deal with theological meaning and contemporary application. Many study guides start with easier questions such as: "To whom is this passage addressed?" "What are the key ideas?" "What did it mean to the people addressed?" Then they proceed to the more complicated questions. In working through the lessons in this study guide, you may want regularly to start with some "easy" factual questions and then move on to the questions of theological interpretation and application to today's problems.

The first lesson may be the most important. Christian concern for the poor should flow out of gratitude for God's acceptance in Christ, not a legalistic sense of dreadful duty. It is crucial that an attitude of loving others "because he first loved us" be established in the first lesson.

The passages selected for each lesson are typical of the other passages in the section of the reader where they are located. Reading all the other related texts for each lesson will help you grasp how much the Scriptures say about a particular topic.

LESSON I: *SERVING OTHERS OUT OF GRATITUDE FOR GOD'S GRACE*

BASIC TEXTS

Rom. 5:6–11; 6:1–14
1 John 4:7–12

QUESTIONS

ROMANS 5:6–11
1. Why does God accept us?
2. How does Christ's death show God's love for us?
3. What kinds of sinners did Christ die for?
4. What does reconciliation with God involve?

ROMANS 6:1–14
1. What does baptism symbolize?
2. Paul says that we *have* died with Christ, that we *shall* live with him, and that we must now consider ourselves dead to sin and alive to God's righteousness. What is the significance of the past and future tenses? Of the simple assertions and the strong commands?
3. How do we walk in newness of life (v. 4) today in our relationships to the poor and hungry?

1 JOHN 4:7–12
1. How do we come to understand the full meaning of love?
2. What should our response be?
3. What does this text tell us about the Christian motivation for concern for the hungry and oppressed?
4. How can we celebrate God's love in our world?

LESSON II: *GOD'S SPECIAL CONCERN FOR THE POOR AT PIVOTAL POINTS OF REVELATION HISTORY*

BASIC TEXTS

Ex. 6:2–9
Amos 4:1–3
Luke 4:16–20

EX. 6:2–9

1. What different reasons are given for God's decision to liberate the Israelite people in Ex. 6:2–9?
2. On the basis of the other texts in this section on revelation history, how central to God's purpose at the exodus was the liberation of oppressed people?
3. Why do you think especially black theologians and Latin American theologians have particularly emphasized the theme of liberation in the biblical teaching on the exodus?

AMOS 4:1–3

1. Why does the prophet denounce the comfortable, well-to-do women? What future does he predict for them?
2. What contact do you think the women had with the poor? What if any was the relationship between their affluent lifestyles and the poor? Is there any parallel to the wives of Mafia leaders or wives of executives in unjust corporations? What obligation do we have to be informed about how others are affected by the way the income to support our lifestyles is earned?

3. As Christians who are saved by grace, how do we apply Amos 4 to ourselves?
4. Do the texts in the section on the destruction of Israel and Judah show the God of the exodus still occupied with the same concerns?

LUKE 4:16–20
1. How does Jesus describe his mission at this public event at the beginning of his ministry?
2. In Luke 7:18ff, John the Baptist asks if Jesus is the expected Messiah. How does Jesus' response (vv. 21–22) correspond with Luke 4:16ff?
3. How does Jesus' description of his mission correspond with the purposes of God discoveᵣed in Ex. 6:2–9 and Amos 4:1–3?

LESSON III: *WHY DOES GOD EXALT THE POOR AND CAST DOWN THE RICH?*

BASIC TEXTS

Luke 1:52–53
Is. 3:13–25
Jer. 5:26–29

QUESTIONS

LUKE 1:52–53
1. On the basis of the texts cited in this lesson, how common a biblical theme is the teaching of Luke 1:53? Do

Christians in affluent nations realize how frequently the Bible teaches this?
2. In the light of the passages in this lesson, why does God cast down the rich and exalt the poor?

IS. 3:13–25; JER. 5:26–29

1. Why according to these passages (especially Is. 3:14 and Jer. 5:26–27) are the rulers rich?
2. When and how are they punished? Do you think that God is at work in history in the same way today?

JAMES 5:1–5

1. This text also says that the rich became rich by oppression. Does this teaching (especially v. 4) have any application to the low wages paid to third world persons who, for example, pick our coffee and bananas?

EZEK. 16:46–50

1. Is there any difference between the actions of the rich people of Sodom and the actions of the rich described in Is. 3:13–25 and Jer. 5:26–29? Is the "sin of omission" committed by the people of Sodom judged any differently from the active oppression condemned in the previous texts in Isaiah, Jeremiah and James?

LESSON IV: *A BIBLICAL WARNING: WHAT IF WE NEGLECT THE POOR?*

BASIC TEXTS

Prov. 14:31
Eccles. 4:1
Is.58:1–10
Matt. 25:31–46

QUESTIONS

PROV. 14:31 AND ECCLES. 4:1

1. Does Eccles. 4:1 help explain why so few people obey Prov. 14:31?
2. Can you see ways in your own life where this happens?

IS. 58:1-10

1. How religious do these people seem to be (see v.2)?
2. Is it possible to be involved in oppression of the poor and still worship God? Is it necessary for every person who wants to worship God to be doing the things described in vv. 6-7?
3. How do you think God views the religious activity and worship of people in rich nations today?
4. How can our worship be a joyful celebration of the God who loves justice and forgives sinners with equal abandon?

MATT. 25:31-46

1. Is it an exaggeration to say that this text teaches that Church members are not Christians at all (regardless of orthodox theology, charismatic experiences, or faithful church attendance) if they do not feed the hungry and care for the poor? How do we relate this text to the biblical teaching that salvation is by grace alone?
2. Who are the people being judged in v.32? Who are the poor (vv.40, 45)? Does thinking about the persons addressed in the preceding verses (Matt. 15:14-30) help?
3. Some interpreters think that this passage (and 1 John 3:17) commands concern only for poor Christians. Does Matt. 5:43-48 (esp. v. 44-45) permit or require us to extend the meaning of Matt. 25 to all poor everywhere?
4. How can we begin to change our lives to implement

our belief that ministering to the hungry and impris-
oned means ministering to Jesus?

LESSON V: *JUBILEE*

BASIC TEXT

Lev. 25:8–17, 23–28

QUESTIONS

LEV. 25:8–17, 23–28

1. Every fifty years all land is to go back to the original
   owners—without compensation. Why did God give
   this command to his people?
2. What is the theological basis for restoration of land
   every fifty years? (See v.23.)
3. What is the basic "capital" in an agricultural society?
4. Why did God give this regular mechanism rather
   than merely depend on the charitable inclinations of
   the rich?
5. Does this passage teach that the right of the original
   owner to have the means to earn a living is a higher
   right than the right of the person with enough money
   to buy the land? (See vv. 24–28.)
6. What does this passage teach about extremes of
   wealth and poverty and about institutionalized
   mechanisms to avoid that?
7. What might be the significance of the fact that the
   year of restoration began on the day of atonement?
   (See v. 9.)
8. What would be some appropriate contempora. ap

plications of this Jubilee passage—in the Church and in secular society?

9. What would an economic system look like that was designed with this Jubilee passage as a fundamental clue to God's will for the economic realm?

10. How does the basic intent of the Old Testament legislation on the sabbatical year, tithing, harvesting and interest in this lesson relate to that of Lev. 25?

11. Does Lev. 25 teach that the right to the resources necessary to earn a living is a higher right than the right to private property? What clues might it offer about how the rich natural resources of nations like the U.S. should be used?

12. What specific things could we begin to do in our individual lives to implement the spirit of Lev. 25?

LESSON VI: *ECONOMIC RELATIONSHIPS IN THE NEW COMMUNITY OF JESUS' FOLLOWERS: SOME EXAMPLES*

BASIC TEXTS

Acts 2:41–47
Acts 4:32–35
Luke 8:1–3
Mark 10:28–31

QUESTIONS

ACTS 2:41–47; 4:32–35

1. What specific things did Christian fellowship include for this body of believers?

2. How extensive was their economic sharing?
3. How accurate would it be to say that, for the Jerusalem church, Christian fellowship involved unlimited economic liability for and unconditional economic availability to the other brothers and sisters in Christ?
4. What should Christian fellowship involve for us today?
5. What was the evangelistic impact of this economic sharing? (See Acts 2:47; 4:33; 6:7.)

LUKE 8:1–3
1. What instances of economic sharing among Jesus' disciples are there in the Gospels? (See also John 12:6; 13:29.)
2. What in the life and teaching of Jesus might have led to the dramatic economic sharing described in Acts 2 and 4?
3. How did the first Christians' sharing grow out of their joyful encounter with God?

MARK 10:28–31
1. What might Jesus have meant by his promise that those who give up everything to follow him will receive a hundred times as much in this present age?
2. Is this promise in Mark 10 related to the economic sharing among Jesus' disciples with the result that the resources of one were available to others as *any had need?* If the Church were living that way today, how would we and others respond to Jesus' words?
3. How might economic relationships within the body of believers be remodeled if we took Lev. 25, Acts 2 and Acts 4 as significant clues to be applied in our very different historical context? How can the Church present a new model of economic sharing that would be relevant to a world divided between rich and poor?

LESSON VII: *PAUL'S COLLECTION FOR JERSUALEM: "THAT THERE MAY BE EQUALITY"*

BASIC TEXT

2 Cor. 8:1-15

QUESTIONS

2 COR. 8:1–15

1. Why does Paul appeal to the example of Jesus in v. 9?
2. What is the guideline for giving presented in vv. 13–15? (Check several other translations. The RSV has a more literal translation of the Greek: "As a *matter of equality* your abundance at the present time should supply their want so that [later] their abundance may supply your want, *that there may be equality.*")
3. How does St Paul's quotation from Ex. 16:18 (in 2 Cor. 8:15) help explain his meaning?
4. What is the significance of the fact that this Pauline collection (unlike the sharing in the Jerusalem church in one locality) was taken in Europe for Christians in Asia?
5. How should St. Paul's guideline of economic equality be applied today in the worldwide body of Christ?
6. By this offering from Gentile Christians to Jewish Christians, Paul meant to speak a word of reconciliation. How might similar sharing be a reconciling action today?
7. Do you see any pattern or patterns in the diverse biblical passages on economic sharing among the people of

God in this lesson? What do these passages tell us about God's attitude toward extremes of wealth and poverty among his people?

LESSON VIII: *MATERIAL ABUNDANCE: CAN THIS GOOD GIFT BE DANGEROUS?*

BASIC TEXTS

Eccles. 9:7
Matt. 6:24–33
Matt. 19:16–26

QUESTIONS

ECCLES. 9:7

1. How does this text reflect the biblical attitude toward creation? (See 1 Tim. 4:4–5; Gen. 1:11–12, 20–22.)
2. How biblical is asceticism?

MATT. 6:24–33

1. What is the secret of this *carefree* attitude toward material possessions?
2. How might the absence of this carefree attitude reflect unbelief (see vv. 26–27, 30) or an unwillingness to accept Jesus as Lord (see vv. 24, 33)?
3. How would the carefree attitude toward possessions advocated by Jesus make us better able to work against hunger and injustice today?

MATT. **19:16–26**

1. Are possessions dangerous? If so, why?
2. What does this word of Jesus say to Christians today?
3. Should most Christians today live a more simple life-style? Why or why not? What relationship might this have to world hunger?
4. How does v. 26 remind us that salvation is by grace?

LESSON IX: *IS MATERIAL ABUNDANCE THE RESULT OF OBEDIENCE?*

BASIC TEXTS

Prov. 6:6–11
Ps.128:1–4
Ps.112:1–5, 9
Prov.18:27

QUESTIONS

PROV. **6:6–11**

1. Is poverty sometimes due to laziness?
2. What does 2 Thes. 3:6–13 tell us about St. Paul's attitude toward laziness?
3. How significant is it that the Bible far more frequently links poverty with oppression than with laziness? (See passages in this lesson and Lesson III.)

PS. **128:1–4**

1. Why does God reward obedience with material abundance? Does he always do that?
2 The Bible tells us both that the world was created good

and that it has been corrupted by the fall. Does the first point help us understand the fact that material abundance is sometimes the result of obedience and the second point suggest why it is not always that way? How?

PS. 112:1–5, 9; PROV. 28:27

1. Do these texts provide any clue about whether one's abundance is the result of oppression or of obedience which God has rewarded?
2. Give your thoughts about the following thesis: "The obedient person obey's God's commands. Many biblical passages demonstrate that one of God's most frequent commands is to have concern for the poor. Therefore those who do not side with the poor can be certain that their material abundance is not the result of God's reward for obedience."
3. At a time when a billion people are malnourished, how affluent should our lifestyle be?

LESSON X: *GOD WILLS JUSTICE*

BASIC TEXTS

Ps.94:1–15
Ex. 13:6–8
Prov. 13:23
Matt. 5:17–20

QUESTIONS

PS. 94:1–15
1. What does this text tell us about the nature of justice?
2. What does this text tell us about the short-term and long-term success of injustice?
3. How does biblical faith provide the necessary hope for the long, costly struggle for justice?

EX. 23:6–8; PROV. 13:23
1. How do these texts tell us more about what justice is?
2. What contemporary illustrations of Prov. 13:23 can you think of?

MATT. 5:17–20
1. In the light of what we know about the content of the Old Testament Law, what does this text say to those who suggest that Jesus had little concern for justice?

LESSON XI: *WHAT ABOUT SYSTEMIC INJUSTICE AND LEGALIZED OPPRESSION?*

BASIC TEXTS

Is. 5:8–16, 22–24
Is. 10:1–4

QUESTIONS

IS. 5:8–16, 22–24

1. Is there any indication that the sin described in v. 8 is illegal. How often is injustice legal?
2. What different kinds of sins are condemned in these verses?
3. Are things like drunkenness more or less sinful than participation in structural sins like economic oppression?
4. Does Amos 2:6–8 reflect the same teaching as Is. 5:8ff? If so, in what way?
5. Do people in rich nations participate in structural sin today?

IS. 10:1–4

1. How does this text add to our understanding of structural sin? (See also Ps. 94:20ff.)
2. Why are unjust laws passed?
3. How similar is this text to the view that laws are merely a reflection of the class interests of the legislators?
4. What warning does God give to societies that legislate injustice? (See also Ps. 94:20ff.)

LESSON XII: *DOES GOD PUNISH UNJUST SOCIETIES?*

BASIC TEXTS

Micah 3:1–4, 9–12
Jer. 22:13–19
Dan. 4:24–28

QUESTIONS

MICAH. 3:1–4, 9–12

1. What does the emotion in this passage convey about the depth of God's passion for justice? How can we feel as deeply?
2. What kinds of injustice are condemned here?
3. In what different ways does God intend to punish them? (See vv. 4 [cf. Amos 8:11–12] and 12 [cf. Jer. 12:7; Amos 6:7].)
4. What is the attitude of the "religious establishment" to the injustice? (See also Amos 7:10–17.) Can you think of modern parallels?

JER. 22:13–19

1. What kinds of injustice are condemned here? Do you know of contemporary examples?
2. What does it mean to know God according to this text? (See especially vv. 15–16.) Does this understanding of the meaning of knowing God correct contemporary Christian thought?
3. Why does God not always punish unjust rulers as promptly as he did King Jehoiakim?

DAN. 4:24–28

1. Does God deal with non-Jewish rulers the same way he did with the kings of Israel?
2. Is God at work in history today pulling down unjust rulers and unjust societies? If so, how?
3. How do you think God views North American society?

LESSON XIII: *AN INVITATION TO STEWARDSHIP AND DISCIPLESHIP*

BASIC TEXTS

Ps. 8:1–9
Matt. 10:37–39
1 Cor. 13:1–3

QUESTIONS

PS.8:1–9
1. How can we celebrate the glory of creation and persons in our work for justice?
2. What is the human mandate for the rest of creation here? (See also Gen. 1:26–31.)
3. Has this mandate been distorted in the industrialized nations? If so, how?
4. What is the relationship of persons to God and the rest of creation and how does this relationship affect our mandate?

MATT. 10:37–39
1. Why did Jesus state the cost of discipleship so harshly?
2. Will there be a cross for those today who follow in Jesus' steps and implement the biblical teaching on the poor and justice? If so, what are some things it might include? Do you have any sense of what that might mean in the next twelve months in your own personal life?
4. We should never forget that the one who calls us so forcefully to costly discipleship is the one who died for

the sins of the world. How can we hold these two truths together without distorting either?

1 COR. 13:1–3
1. What does Paul mean by love? How can our lives overflow with that kind of love?
2. Persons who become passionately concerned about justice and simple living sometimes become harsh and self-righteous. What does this passage tell us about how we should relate to others who do not yet share that concern?

LESSON XIV: *GENERAL SUGGESTIONS FOR FINAL CLASS*

---

1. Have each person make a list of the ways God is calling him or her to costly discipleship in light of this series of lessons.
2. Make a list together of how family units could live more simply.
3. Make a list of the ways your congregation and the larger Church could live more simply.
4. How can you use your influence as a Christian citizen to help eliminate some of the causes of hunger and help bring justice to the poor?
5. Make a list of all the organizations you know that are working to implement the concerns of these lessons. (You may obtain a list of some of these groups by writing to Bread for the World, 32 Union Square E., New York, N.Y. 10003.)
6. Ask what support structure in your local congregation is needed to help people begin to implement their changed values and new concerns.
7. Give people an opportunity to make plans for an ongoing prayer/fellowship/study/action group.

BIBLICAL INDEX

218

219